Meet the Big Cats!

Cover image: Matt Gibson/Shutterstock

For Nessa, whose broad grin and unconditional love helped me through some dark places.

TABLE OF CONTENTS

Forward

What do you know about big cats?

That they're awesome, yes. Also, that they're endangered.

And big cats are scary, too, since they're large enough to harm someone if they attack.

But do they always attack us? No; they often try to avoid humans.

Are big cats at all like house cats? Yes, in many ways!

How many are there? At least six species: lions, tigers, leopards, jaguars, snow leopards, and clouded leopards.

Where do big cats live, and what are they like? Ah, now

we're getting into the subject of this book.

I've assumed that laypeople like me want to know as much as possible about big cats. That's why I've written this book -- to introduce them to you.

There is a lot of information here, collected from scientific papers and authoritative online sources like the Cat Specialist Group, which I've tried to translate from jargon into plain English.

It may seem a little overwhelming. That's why there are also lots of images of these beautiful felines, as well as links to a few online videos that feature big cats and to some interesting websites. (*These links are live in the eBook but will be listed at the end of each chapter here; they're current as of early December 2019. Try the Internet Archive's Wayback Machine for web pages that may have changed since then.*)

I hope that eventually the text will win out, becoming a window for you to really see big cats for the first time.

And that's not all. I want to pique your curiosity, too.

Check out the reference section at the end of the book!

No, seriously, fact-check me. I'm only a layperson, after all, and might have inserted bias and/or misunderstood something a scientist wrote.

But mostly I hope that you'll use those references to get even more information about big cats and the state of human knowledge about Panthera.

To keep this book short and accessible to laypeople, there is very little technical stuff in it about complicated matters such as home range sizes and food-web interactions, even though these are a huge part of any wild cat's existence.

You'll find information galore about such things in the references. These include website links; scientific papers that you might find online via Google Scholar or a rental service like DeepDyve (my two main sources) or a local university library (I owe many thanks to Price and Knight libraries, at the University of Oregon, and Valley Library, at Oregon State University, for their making so much useful information available to the general public!).

If you do spot an error or have any questions, drop me a line at bjdeming at gmail.com.

And thank you very much for your interest!

Corvallis, Oregon

November 26, 2019

Tambako The Jaguar, CC BY-ND 2.0 https://www.flickr.com/photos/tambako/34948585636

Lions

This beloved wild cat needs no introduction.

However, it might surprise you to hear that, under the skin, the King and Queen of Beasts are really just scaled-up house cats! (*Turner and Antón*).

And when it comes to behavior, lions have a lot in common with Fluffy, the king of our hearts.

For instance:

- In both species, related females group together in a social unit. With Fluffy, that's called a colony (with a few males that live on the periphery); in lions, it's a pride (males are much more dominant here).
- Both lionesses and she-cats help out with birth and then share nursery duties when raising their cubs and kittens, respectively.
- Lions and tomcats vocalize at the right frequency to be heard far away. However, size does matter: that lion's roar carries up to six miles, while a tomcat's yowl is only audible for about a quarter mile.

Of course, there are major differences, too, and not just those that show up on general inspection.

This brings us to the basic question: House cats we know, but what exactly *is* a lion?

Scientific name: *Panthera leo.*

Lions have two recognized subspecies.

1. The one most of us know, the African lion (*P. leo leo*).

2. But India has a lion, too -- the rare Asiatic or Gir lion (*P. leo persica*).

These subspecies are much alike. Asiatic lions are smaller than their African counterparts, and males often have a skin flap on their bellies, as well as sparser manes.

Asiatic lion in Berlin zoo, by avda-foto, CC BY-SA 2.0. https://www.flickr.com/photos/93015232@N04/24340997809

Data

This information is from the Cat Specialist Group website (see source list), except where noted. There is quite a number spread in each category because lions are much bigger than lionesses.

African lion:

- **Adult weight:** 240 to 600 pounds.

- **Height at the shoulder:** 3 to 4 feet (*Sunquist and Sunquist*)

- **Body length:** 4-1/2 to 8 feet.

- **Tail length:** 2 to a little over 3 feet.

- **Coat:** Adults have solid-colored short fur, light tan to silvery gray, yellowish red, or dark brown. Cubs often have spots, and occasional faint belly markings show in some adult females. The cat's underside is generally a paler version of the overall coat color. We'll look at the mane a little later in this chapter. (*Sunquist and Sunquist*) Sometimes, particularly in southern Africa, a genetic mutation produces lions with a white or blonde coat. These aren't albinos -- they just never developed the usual dark pigments that combine with lighter ones to make the typical lion fur colors.

(*Cincinnati Zoo*)

- Litter size: 1 to 4 cubs.

- Average life span: 12 to 16 years. (I think the Cat
  Specialist Group includes captive animals in these
  figures; life in the wild is hard enough to shorten a
  lion's life expectancy.)

Asiatic lion:

- Weight: 240 to 420 pounds.

- Body length: 4-1/2 to 8 feet.

- Tail length: 2 to a little over 3 feet.

- Litter size: 1 to 4 cubs.

- Average life span: 16 to 18 years.

Features unique to lions

- Mane and tail tassel: Whether it's yellow, brown, or reddish brown, the mane usually starts to grow as a young lion matures, at around age 3-1/2; then it darkens and thickens with age. (*Sunquist and Sunquist*) The Asiatic lion's mane isn't as impressive as its African counterpart, but in cooler climates this subspecies does grow a thick mane. (*Loveridge et al., 2010b*) Asiatic lions have the longest tail tassel, though. (They also typically have a thick fold of belly skin, unlike African lions.) This tuft of hair first appears when a lion or lioness is about 5-1/2 months old. Sometimes it covers a bony knob that protrudes slightly from the end of the tail. It looks to us as though lions use their highly visible tail tassel for communication and/or identification, but since we don't know Leo's point of view, there will always remain some uncertainty about why lions have this unique feature.

- The pride: Lions are the only cat that's *this* social. The number of members and other details vary quite a lot from place to place and even from pride to pride. In every group, related adult lionesses form the core. There may be, on average, 4 or 5 lionesses per pride in India's Gir National Park and up to 18 out on the Serengeti. (*Sunquist and Sunquist*) Accompanying lionesses are either growing cubs or subadults. Adult males come and go (on average, there are 2 to 6 males per pride in Gir and 1 to 7 in Serengeti prides, per Sunquist and Sunquist); the "king" reigns for some 24 to 36 months before usurpers come along (*Cat Specialist Group*), though some male coalitions can hold onto a pride for a long time.

- ROAR! Yes, some other big cats also make the hills and forests ring, but according to Kitchener *et al.* (2010), sonograms show that only lions do a completely structured call series. Leopards and jaguars show a few pieces of the pattern. Tigers just have the main call and grunt.

Where found in the wild

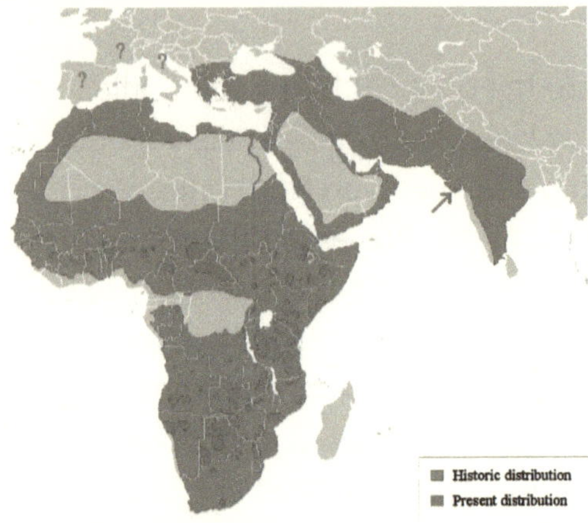

Historically, lions were once widespread across all of Africa and much of Europe, the Middle East, and southern Asia.

That's the red part of this image by Tommyknocker via Wikimedia https://commons.wikimedia.org/wiki/File:Lion_distributio n.png#mw-jump-to-license

P. leo leo, the African lion, is found in various habitats south of the Sahara, mainly savanna lands that support numerous prey animals and provide just enough open woodlands for lions to shelter in and use as cover.

Experts aren't sure how many wild lions live here now. There might be around 20,000 to 30,000, mostly in southern and eastern Africa, with more than half of these in conservation areas. (*Cat Specialist Group; Macdonald et al., 2010a*)

P. leo persica used to roam all of southwestern Asia. Now, the only wild Asiatic lions live in and around Gir Park in Gujarat State, India. (*Cat Specialist Group*)

Closest cat family relatives

Most molecular studies of big cat DNA reportedly show that lions are a little more closely related to jaguars and leopards than they are to tigers and snow leopards. (*Christiansen; Kitchener et al., 2017*)

Some experts link leopards and lions together, while others argue that jaguars are the lion's "sister."

That latter claim might sound far-fetched, since jaguars and lions now live on completely different continents.

However, the fossil record shows that lions did reach the

New World, perhaps getting down as far as northern South America before they eventually went extinct in this part of the world.

They probably arrived during the ice ages, when a huge drop in global sea level turned what's now the Bering Strait into dry land.

Famous lions

We have used the lion image in many different cultural ways.

For example:

The Belfort lion, in Europe. It inspired an essay by English writer G. K. Chesterton nine years before the outbreak of World War I (included in his book, "Tremendous Trifles").

In real life, human-lion connections are intense, whether we're running for our lives, admiring this cat's majestic appearance and roar, or reaching out to embrace them.

- Man-eaters. Each year, someone falls prey to wild lions, particularly in Tanzania. There also have been a few mass outbreaks in the past. Perhaps the most infamous man-eaters were the 19th-century Tsavo lions, although the early 20th-century attacks in Njombe had a reportedly higher body count.

- More likeable lions include the MGM lions -- yes, it's

plural. There's only one lion shown roaring in the MGM logo at the start of a movie, but several cats have had the gig. Nowadays we're looking at **Leo**, who first appeared in the 1950s. He was preceded by **George**, **Tanner**, **Coffee**, **Telly**, and **Slats** (who originated the role a century ago)

- **Elsa:** In the 1950s, Elsa and her sisters **Big One** and **Lustica** were just a few days old when game warden George Adamson was forced to shoot their mother, who charged him when he unwittingly got too close to the den. The Adamson's cared for the three cubs. Big One and Lustica were adopted by a Dutch zoo, but as documented in *Born Free* and its sequels, Elsa was trained to survive in the wild and then released.

- **Christian:** You've probably seen videos like this one about the lion cub that was born in captivity, purchased by two young London men from Harrod's, and eventually, with the help of George Adamson, successfully released back into the wild at Kenya's Kora National Reserve. What you might not have realized is that this all happened in the early 1970s! Videos of the first reunion, in either 1971 or 1972, between Christian and the two men who raised him went viral in the early 2000s and left the impression that it had just happened. But long before that, Christian had returned to the wild and was never seen again.

- Prosperity, official mascot of the US Senate: In 1998, Siegfried & Roy donated a group of white lions to the Cincinnati Zoo, including **Prosperity, Sunshine** and **Future.** Wikipedia has a list of other well-known white lions, a color mutation. These pretty cats aren't albinos -- they just lack dark pigmentation.

How lions live in the wild

Lions are usually active right after sunset and before dawn, and perhaps also around midnight.

Aaaaand -- that's about it, as this image by TTphoto/Shutterstock shows. These dozy cats have been known to sleep for 24 hours after a heavy meal!

In the wild, they nap 14 to 20 hours or more each day. For captive lions, that's "only" 10 to 15 hours.

When it's time to eat, a lion will chow down on almost anything up to and including ostrich eggs. However, these hypercarnivores generally go after medium to large hoofed plant-eaters, ranging from water buffalo to warthogs.

Why do lions form prides?

We all assume that it's so they can catch more prey by working together.

After all, per Ewer (see reference list at the end of this book), lionesses have been observed:

- Fanning out to flush prey out of cover
- Circling around and chasing prey toward another lioness who's waiting in ambush
- Herding prey into a cul-de-sac (don't laugh -- several animals do this)

But even these clever cats only have about a 30% success rate, tops. (*Sunquist and Sunquist*)

Zoologists have yet to unquestionably prove a connection between lion society and hunting.

Perhaps living together helps lions defend their food. (*Macdonald and et al., 2010a*) After all, they operate out in the open, where scavenging is a big problem.

Not shown: All the scavengers attracted by the "dinner bell." (Peter Schwarz/Shutterstock)

Enough hyenas, for example, may gather to drive lionesses away from a carcass. But if the pride's much larger lions are around, those scavengers are out of luck. (*Macdonald and et al., 2010a*)

There *is* an evolutionary down side to such group defense, though.

A single carcass only goes so far, and competition for a feeding spot is intense. In large prides, youngsters often get pushed aside, even when Mom tries to make room for them.

If that happens too often, the pride will have traded away their future for just one meal in the here and now.

How lions reproduce

Lions mate at any time of year. Once pregnant, a lioness doesn't come into heat again until her cubs mature, about 24 months after birth, or are killed during a pride takeover (a brutal fact of life in lion country).

Newborns weigh 2 to 3 pounds. Their eyes generally are

open at birth, or soon afterwards.

A housecat's kittens are usually weaned by eight weeks and are independent from Mom at around six months of age. This whole process takes about four times as long for lion cubs.

That's not surprising, given their larger size and the whole "apex predator" thing. It takes a while for juveniles to learn how to survive on their own.

It takes a while for a full mane to grow in. Nevertheless, adolescent certainly have presence, as this image by Tambako the Jaguar, CC BY-ND 2.0,

https://www.flickr.com/photos/tambako/26797989623,
shows.

Finally, it's time to leave home.

As with other feline moms, the pride's lionesses may allow
females to settle in. Subadult males usually leave to make
their own way in the world.

Wandering young lions often form coalitions.

For a while, they'll hone their hunting and other survival
skills, but at around age four years, they start looking for a
pride.

This leads to some intense confrontations.

Sometimes the resident male of the pride wins.
Sometimes he does not. When this happens, the new
lions drive out all the subadult males and, sadly, kill all the
cubs so that they can sire their own offspring.

Almost a third of all lion cubs on the Serengeti die this way before reaching maturity. It's a horribly efficient way to ensure that only the fittest lions pass along their genes. (*Macdonald et al., 2010a*)

Interactions with people

We've already looked at this a little bit (the chapter on lions in Sunquist and Sunquist has even more fascinating historical details).

Basically, as Loveridge *et al.* (2010a) note, there are two very different kinds of interaction between lions and people:

1. Lions may be cultural icons, as well as tourist attractions and conservation symbols.

2. They are also a threat, preying on livestock and on us. In Tanzania, for example, almost 600 people were killed, and hundreds more injured, between 1990 and 2004; and from 1978 to 1991, Gir lions killed 28 and injured 165 people, mainly near the preserve rather than in it.

People also overexploit lions, steal their prey for bushmeat, and break up their habitat.

For most readers, this talk about predation and exploitation are intellectual problems, but for anyone living near a preserve -- especially a subsistence farmer who really can't afford to lose livestock and is afraid to let the children outdoors to play -- it's a very serious concern.

Surprisingly, many locals -- especially in India, for cultural reasons -- try to work with conservationists and other stakeholders.

Cost-effective measures like guards or simply putting livestock inside a building overnight do work. But it's very difficult to get everyone on board with lion conservation, especially if they have suffered losses or personal harm.

Yet local support is vital -- it only takes one aggrieved person, using weapons and/or poison, to wipe out an entire lion pride.

Red-listed?

- **African lions:** Vulnerable. More information:
  https://www.iucnredlist.org/species/15951/1151304
  19

- **Asiatic lions:** Endangered. More information:
  https://www.iucnredlist.org/species/15952/5327221
  (The good news is that conservationists believe this
  population, though tiny, is stable.)

Fossil relatives

While lions have a good fossil history, compared to some
other pantherines, their evolution is still mostly a mystery.

For example, researchers have found four-million-year-old
fossils from a large lion-like cat in Tanzania, but no one yet
knows if the world's oldest lion.

There simply isn't enough evidence yet to clearly indicate
how that ancient predator was connected to today's big
cats. (*Werdelin and Dehghani*)

Confirmed lion fossils are all less than two million years old, although molecular markers indicate that lions and other big cats go back at least ten million years. (*Werdelin et al.*)

Herding fossil lions is not easy.

> *Lion taxonomy has long been controversial. Some authorities place all fossil lions in the modern species, "P. leo," while others recognize a number of extinct species, for example, "P. spelea," the cave lion, and "P. atrox," the North American lion.*
>
> *-- Werdelin et al.*

We do have eyewitness descriptions of *P. spelea* from around 30,000 years ago.

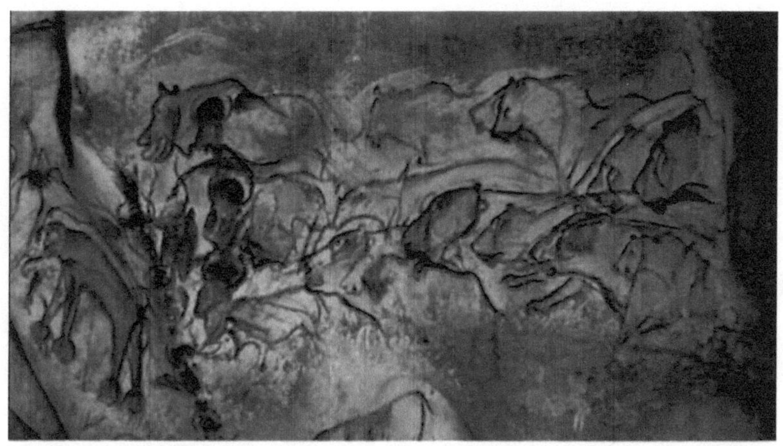

"P. spelea", as depicted by early humans on the walls of France's Chauvet Cave Note the lack of a mane: was this a group of lionesses or were cave lions mane-less?
https://commons.wikimedia.org/wiki/File:Lions_group_Chauvet_Cave.jpg

Spelea's fossils have been found from England to China.

It may have sheltered in caves but it also prowled the mammoth steppe -- an open ecosystem that was sort of like a savanna but with bears, mammoths, and other creatures that you're not ever going to see on the Serengeti.

"P. atrox" (right) and one of the neighborhood cats -- Smilodon. (Image: Joe Mabel, via Wikimedia, CC BY-SA 3.0) https://commons.wikimedia.org/wiki/File:California_Sabre-tooth_%26_American_Lion_01.jpg

Isotopic analysis suggests that the cave lion's favorite food was reindeer/caribou, although it could only dominate the food web in areas where the climate was too cold for other big carnivores. (*Bocherens*)

When reindeer and caribou headed into the Arctic as the last Ice age wound down, Spelea did not follow them. Instead, it went extinct some 11,000 years ago.

Fossils of *P. atrox*, the North American lion (though some experts, like Christiansen, disagree with that classification), were first found in Natchez, Mississippi, in the late 1850s.

This big cat roamed North America during the late Pleistocene, roughly 50,000 years ago. There were other large cats around then, including sabertooths, but little is known about their ecology.

One possibility is that Atrox prowled pine parklands in northern parts of the continent, leaving warmer areas, like what are now Florida and Texas, to prehistoric jaguars. (*Martin and Neuner*)

By this time, modern lions were present. How could they coexist with these impressive relatives?

Some researchers hypothesize that, in ice age times:

- Leo (the modern lion) held sway in Africa and southwestern Eurasia

- Spelea (the cave lion) ranged from Europe across northern Eurasia to Alaska (via the Bering Land Bridge).

- Atrox (the North American lion) was centered in what's now the southern United States.

However these ancient lion species may have shared the land, Leo was the only lion left standing after the Ice Age. And modern lions are hanging in there still today.

Asiatic lion numbers in India, while low, have doubled over the last 10 years.

In Africa, conservationists, governments, and local people are committed to finding ways to protect lions and the human beings who must live alongside them.

There's hope for the future. But only time can tell what's in store next for all stakeholders in this difficult work.

Hyperlinks

- *Video*: Asiatic (Gir) lions: https://youtu.be/6sexdHPVBMQ

- *Web page*: Messy Beast on the genetics of white lions: http://messybeast.com/genetics/lions-white.htm

- *Video*: Lion roaring: https://youtu.be/1e0_4dwF9A4

- *Web page*: The Tsavo man-eating lions: https://www.sciencemag.org/news/2009/11/body-count-two-man-eating-lions

- *Web page*: The Njombe man-eaters: http://www.naturalhistorymag.com/0509/0509_feature.html?page=3

- *Web page*: Wikipedia, MGM lion: https://en.wikipedia.org/wiki/Leo_the_Lion_(MGM)

- *Video*: Christian the Lion: https://youtu.be/btuxO-C2IzE

- *Web page*: Wikipedia, White lions: https://en.wikipedia.org/wiki/White_lion

- *Video*: Lion prides and "hot spots": https://youtu.be/zobZd8Mp3sk

- *Video*: Two lions challenge a resident male: https://youtu.be/BjByTjOkyi0

- *Video*: Two lionesses charge a game-reserve fence: https://youtu.be/w5mTcYKeePo

- *Video*: Local resident decides to help conservation efforts: https://youtu.be/Ai9ZnPt-jjs

Heather Smithers CC BY-SA 2.0 https://www.flickr.com/photos/36107339@N03/34822683924

Tigers

Even at rest, tigers convey a sense of power.

Yet there's also something there that makes us want to hug them or, more safely, to anthropomorphize tigers in toys and artwork.

Perhaps it's that adorable white-furred muzzle; those intricate facial markings (unique to each individual); the gaudy coat; the round head with its cute little ears.

Whatever is going on, this big cat definitely holds a special place -- tinged with fear, love, and respect -- in human hearts.

Scientific name: *Panthera tigris.*

This applies to Royal Bengal, Siberian, and other kinds of tiger you might have heard of.

White tigers like these (photographed by Jack Fiallos, CC BY 2.0, https://www.flickr.com/photos/erlingfiallos/500979330) are Royal Bengals with a color mutation.

However, there's an ongoing debate in scientific circles about subspecies -- for instance, calling Bengal tigers *P. tigris tigris*.

That's not incorrect; *P. tigris tigris* has been the formal moniker of Bengal tigers for a long time.

What's controversial is that some taxonomists now want it to include other subgroups. They believe that there are just two tiger subspecies.

That's getting pretty esoteric for those of us who aren't sure what the difference is between, say, a Bengal and a Siberian tiger (other than location).

Here's an overview of how scientists classify tigers at present:

<u>Traditional tiger subspecies</u>

Data often varies from source to source. I've used the Cat Specialist Group for geographic information unless otherwise noted. Estimated numbers are from Luo et al. (2004) except where noted.

- Royal Bengal tiger (*Panthera tigris tigris*): More information: http://www.catsg.org/index.php?id=564 India, Bangladesh, Bhutan, western China, western Myanmar, and Nepal. (*Luo et al.*) Estimated number in the wild, 2004: 3,200 to 4,500.

- Amur/Siberian tiger (*P. t. altaica*): More information: http://www.catsg.org/index.php?id=567 Mostly in the Russian Far East, with a few in northeastern China and possibly some also in North Korea, though that hasn't yet been verified. It's reportedly the only tiger found in snowy areas, although Goodrich *et al.* note that Bengal tigers have been seen at elevations up to 15,000 feet in Bhutan. Estimated number in the wild, 2004: Fewer than 500. It could be worse. Wild Amur/Siberian tigers had a brush with extinction in the 1930s, when they may have been down to their last 20 or 30 individuals. Since then, Soviet and Russian conservationists have had some success in bringing these beautiful big cats back.

- Sumatran tiger (*P. t. sumatrae*): More information: http://www.catsg.org/index.php?id=568 Only on the island of Sumatra, in Indonesia. This is the world's smallest tiger (though it's still a very big cat!). Estimated number in the wild, 2004: 400 to 500.

- Indochinese tiger (*P. t. corbetti*): More information: http://www.catsg.org/index.php?id=565 Southeast Asia north of the Malayan Peninsula. Estimated number in the wild, 2004: 1,200 to 1,800.

- Malayan tiger (*P. t. jacksoni*): More information: http://www.catsg.org/index.php?id=572 Peninsular Malaysia. Estimated number in the wild, 2010: 493 to 1,480. (*Cat Specialist Group*)

- Amoy/South China tiger (*P. t. amoyensis*): More information: http://www.catsg.org/index.php?id=566 Probably extinct in the wild; none observed since the 1970s. Estimated number in the wild, 2004: Extinct. There are still some 50 Amoy/South China tigers in captivity.

An additional three subspecies went extinct recently (*Luo et al.*):

- Bali tigers (*P. t. balica*) in the 1940s

- Caspian tigers (*P. t. virgata*) in the 1970s (but see Culver *et al.*)

- Java tigers (*P. t. sondaica*) in the 1980s

How are the surviving tiger subspecies different from one another?

Not very much, actually.

Some of these subspecies (notably, the Malayan and Amoy/South China tigers) can only recognized genetically -- on the outside, they all resemble one another.

This is why some boffins want to divvy up tigers into only two groups: mainland Asia and the Sunda Islands, which include Sumatra, Java, and Bali.

<u>Proposed tiger subspecies</u>

- Mainland tigers (*P. t. tigris*). Bengal tigers, but also Amur/Siberian, Malayan, Indochinese, and Amoy tigers; the extinct Caspian tigers are in this group, too, because scientific names represent evolution and descent, not just who's left standing at a particular point in geological time.

- Sunda tigers (*P. t. sondaica*). Sumatran tigers, along

with the extinct Java and Bali cats.

That's it -- a much simpler setup overall but lacking the close regional associations that many tigers now have.

The reasoning is that these islands were once dry land -- an extension of the Asian continent called Sundaland -- back during the ice ages. Tigers wandered in there, became isolated after the ice melted and sea levels rose, and evolved a little differently from those on the mainland.

Indeed, some experts say that something like this appears to have happened already with clouded leopards, as we'll see towards the end of this book.

Other boffins, however, argue against this mainland/Sunda tiger business. They find enough genetic and physical differences between subgroups to justify the traditional subspecies list.

There are good arguments both for and against each of the above points.

Data

This information is from the Cat Specialist Group website unless otherwise noted. (Image: catlovers CC BY-SA 2.0

https://www.flickr.com/photos/90389546@N00/3512034897)

Lion data are included for comparison because tropical tigers may be smaller than lions, though individual Amur/Siberian and Bengal tigers are indeed the world's biggest cats.

- **Weight:** 165 to 716 pounds (Lions: 243 to 600 pounds).

- **Height at shoulder:** 2.3 to 4 feet (African lion: 3 to 4 feet). (*Sunquist and Sunquist; Wikipedia*)

- Body length: 5 to 7.6 feet. (Lions: 4.5 to 8.2 feet.)

- Tail length: 3 to 3.6 feet. (Lions: 2 to 3.3 feet)

- Coat: The background color is usually rusty red to yellow-orange.   Reports of melanistic (all black) tigers haven't been verified, but white tigers with are well known. Late in the 20th century, zoos banned breeding of white tigers, as many health problems were showing up, but in 2013 Xu *et al.* reported that white coloration is just a normal tiger color variation; associated health problems were probably due to intensive inbreeding of captives to get more white tigers. Pure black or brownish stripes (dark sepia in white tigers) vary in number, shape, and direction -- the pattern is unique to each tiger. The back of each ear is black except for a very noticeable white spot that tigers probably use for signalling. If you ever catch a tiger by the tail, or even if not, be sure to admire those dark rings on it and the tail's black tip. Males, especially on Sumatra, have a prominent ruff (not a mane), and northern tigers develop a fairly shaggy winter coat -- up to 2.5 inches deep -- that can be long enough to hide their small, round ears! For comparison, a Bengal tiger's coat is typically less than an inch thick. (*Ewer, Heptner and Sludskii; Kitchener et al. [2010]; Schneider et al.; Wikipedia; Xu et al.*)

- Vocals: Tigers make most of the typical feline sounds except purring. Yes, tigers do occasionally meow! When it comes to roaring, though, studies show that they only do part of the full sequence that lions perform. Another unusual sound tigers make is the chuff (also called a prusten). This extended breathy grunt, typically used in social situations, is something only tigers, clouded leopards, snow leopards, and jaguars do. They also grunt and, when feeling tense, tigers moan. (*Christiansen; Kitchener et al., 2010; Sunquist and Sunquist; Wikipedia*)

- Average litter size: 1 to 5; typically, per Ewer, 2 to 3.

- Average life span: 12 to 15 years. The Amur Tiger Center reports that these cats live up to 15 years in the wild and up to 20 years in captivity.

Features unique to tigers

- As this image by Tambako the Jaguar, CC BY-ND 2.0

  https://www.flickr.com/photos/tambako/664757839 5 shows, Bengal tigers have the **longest fangs in the modern cat family.** (*Heske*) However, as we'll see towards the end of this book, another member of Panthera takes that record when you factor in body size.

- As mentioned above, some Amur/Siberian and Bengal tigers are the **largest members of today's cat family.**

- Stripes! There are no spotted tigers. (*Werdelin and Olsson*) People use striping patterns to tell individual tigers apart, but no one knows if the cat uses them this way. Some experts suggest that vertical stripes help tigers blend into a background of grass, but this might not be the case. (*Allen et al.*) One team found that this coat pattern has a "spatial frequency" that's similar to most backgrounds (in other words, stripes blur the tiger as it sneaks up on prey or hides in ambush). But if that's true, then why aren't most predators striped? (*Godfrey et al.*)

- Tigers may have the shortest developmental branch of any member of the cat family. (*Cho et al.; Culver et al.; Haslam and Petraglia; Williams*) Their genetic "reset button" has been hit a few times in the last 100,000 years. (*Cho et al.*) No one knows for sure what caused this, although many hypotheses have been proposed.

Where found in the wild

Tigers evolved to hunt and kill large hoofed animals. (*Cat Specialist Group*)

Like all members of family Felidae, they'll eat almost anything they come across. But when the big ungulates disappear, so do tigers. (*Sunquist and Sunquist*)

And ungulates are disappearing.

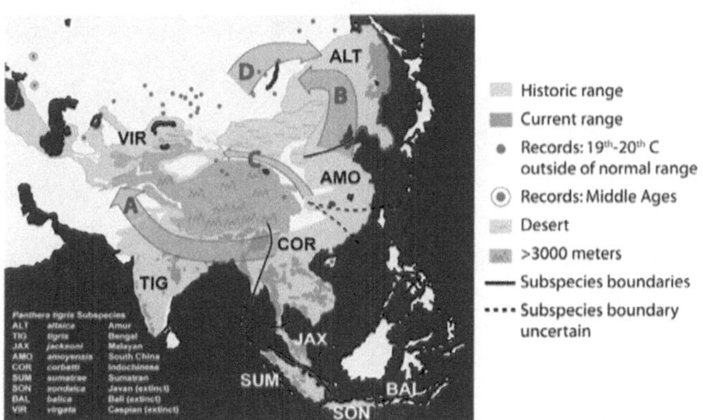

Figure 1: Driscoll, C. A.; Yamaguchi, N.; Bar-Gal, G. K.; Roca, A. L.; and others. 2009 Mitochondrial phylogeography illuminates the origin of the extinct Caspian Tiger and its relationship to the Amur tiger. PLoS ONE 4(1): e4125. https://journals.plos.org/plosone/article?id=10.1371/journal.pone.0004125 Public domain.

People hunt and eat animals like deer and wild boar, too. And as the human population of tiger country has increased, we have also cleared the land and brought in domestic livestock, driving away even more of the tiger's natural prey.

Hunting these big cats for sport and profit, or for cultural reasons like traditional Asian medicine, has also sent tigers into a steep decline.

All of this is why the the Caspian, Java, and Bali tigers are extinct, and why there no longer are tigers in much of southwestern and central Asia.

It's a depressing picture. But there *are* still wild tigers.

Increasing their numbers is one of the biggest challenges conservationists face today. (*Seidensticker et al.*)

But such efforts work better now that everyone knows that this involves not only counting big white-whiskered feline noses but also keeping "tiger country" as intact as possible -- with dense cover, much water, and lots of prey.

We've already gotten a general idea of where tigers are the list of subspecies, but what does tiger country look like on the ground?

- For one thing, there is always **dense** cover, whether it's the reed jungles of Nepal's Terai (a floodplain at the base of the Himalayas that hosts more tigers per square mile than anywhere else in the world); thick

stands of oak and other deciduous trees in the
Russian Far East (wherever snow doesn't get more
than about a foot and a half deep in winter); mangrove
swamps of the Sundarbans in India and Bangladesh;
or the subtropical and tropical forests of Southeast
Asia.

- Water is a must, too. Tigers like to cool off in pools
  during hot weather and they're also excellent
  swimmers -- Heptner and Sludskii note that Amur
  tigers have even strayed across the four-mile-wide
  Tartary Strait to reach Sakhalin Island off Russia's
  Pacific coast!

- Water attracts the big cat's main prey: large ungulates,
  as hoofed plant-eaters like deer and wild boar are
  called. You see many of these hefty herbivores (200
  pounds or more) in good "tiger country," despite the
  fact that a single cat eats 50 or more each year.
  (*Seidensticker et al.*)

Closest cat family relatives

Panthera is the oldest group in the modern cat family, but molecular studies have shown something surprising about tigers and another pantherine: the snow leopard.

While not everyone goes along with this (*Christiansen*), many researchers think that snow leopards and tigers are very closely related, even though they don't look very much alike on the outside. (*Kitchener et al., 2017*)

Famous tigers

- A few fictional tigers that most Westerners will recognize are **Hobbes** (cartoon), **Tigger** (Winnie the Pooh books), **Daniel Striped Tiger** (Mister Rogers' TV show), and **Shere Khan** (*The Jungle Book*).

- **Genghis**. You might not have heard of this real-life Bengal tiger, a resident of India's Ranthambore Park. In the 1980s, per Turner and Antón, Genghis worked out a new way to hunt deer. He waited until they were in the water and then rushed in, distracting them with the splashes. This approach had never been reported in over two centuries of tiger observations there.

- Mohan. Mohan is the ancestor of almost all of today's captive white tigers. A Bengal tiger captured in 1951, he's also the last known wild-born white tiger, although others have been reported in India since at least the 1500s. (Xu *et al.*) Mohan passed away in 1970.

- Siegfried and Roy's white tigers, including Mantecore, who mauled Roy in 2003 but was not blamed for the attack (Mantecore died in 2014 at age 17 after a brief illness). The two entertainers have retired, but their white tigers, with a new generation present now, continue to appear as an attraction in Siegfried and Roy's Secret Garden and Dolphin Habitat at The Mirage.

- Artiom, Boris and Svetlaya, Vladik, Philippa, Saikhan, and the Tigress From Lazo: You might not have heard of them, but these Amur tigers, successfully reintroduced to the wild between 2014 and 2018, are very popular among Russian conservationists. (*Amur*

Tiger Center)

How tigers hunt and live

Tigers are stalk-and-ambush hunters, like all cats. They'll
either wait for prey to come along or slink into position as
close as possible to their target before attacking (while
tigers can jump 20 feet or more, Ewer notes that no one
has ever observed them leaping onto prey)

A short chase may ensue, but tigers are not pursuit
predator. They wrestle prey to the ground, dispatching
ungulates and other large prey with a throat bite that
keeps the tiger clear of flying hoofs or horns. Smaller prey
are killed with a spine-severing bite to the back of the neck.

On average, just one in five hunts is successful. That's a
lower success rate than lions have, but the kill is usually
large enough to provide several meals for a single
predator.

Tigers also use dense
natural to cache food while

they rest nearby, well hidden by vegetation and trees.

They aren't quite as dozy as lions, but tigers generally get in a solid 12 hours of sleep each day. (Image: Koshy Koshy, CC BY 2.0, https://www.flickr.com/photos/kkoshy/3503896744)

Of note, though all cats are considered solitary predators, multiple tigers have been seen feeding at a kill, some of them unrelated!

And occasionally several tigers will gather together and hang out for a while even when it's not breeding season. No one understands what is going on in these get-togethers, but it might be similar to the sociability that domestic cats sometimes show. (*Ewer; Turner and Antón*)

Given this apparent friendliness, why isn't there, say, a "magnificence" of tigers, just as there is a pride of lions?

Perhaps because tigers don't live in open lands, as lions do, and therefore scavenging isn't such a threat to them. (*Macdonald et al, 2010a*)

How tigers reproduce

Like all cats, male tigers base their territory around females, while the females are more concerned with having enough prey in their territory to support themselves as well as their cubs. (Image of two tigers snuggling is by Tambako the Jaguar, CC BY-ND 2.0, https://www.flickr.com/photos/tambako/15426516173)

The Cat Specialist Group reports that the only known breeding tiger populations are in Bangladesh, Bhutan, India, Indonesia, Malaysia, Nepal, Russia, and Thailand.

Between 2009 and 2014, they say, a few tigers with cubs were also seen in China and Myanmar.

Breeding seasons vary by region. After about three months, tiger cubs are born, weighing 2 to 4 pounds. They have the same striped coat as adults. Some are born with their eyes open, though it may take up to three weeks to open their eyes.

 Youngsters grow fast, often quadrupling their weigh in the first month. (Image by Mathias Appel, public domain https://www.flickr.com/photos/mathiasappel/304602020 82) The cubs first taste meat at around age three months, but there's a lot of individual variation in how tigers develop.

Family relationships can be complex, too.

For example, sources differ on Dad's role in raising the cubs. Some report that male tigers have very little to do with it. Others note that males will protect their cubs, and one report even described a male tiger raising his cubs to maturity after their mother died!

However, Miquelle *et al.* say that Amur and Bengal tigers in their study had similar reproduction parameters, despite the very different natural conditions these two cats experience.

Tiger cubs typically start accompanying their mother on hunts when they're two months old, but at first they don't participate. They wait until Mom calls them to the kill.

Around age four months, the cubs are the size of an Irish setter and very playful. Two months later, they're fully weaned but still have a lot to learn about surviving as a predator.

It will take another 12 to 18 months before the young tigers are ready for life on their own. And they'll continue to grow until reaching their full adult size at about age five.

Interactions with people

We've very briefly mentioned some of the special connections people feel with tigers, as well as the pride that various parts of the world have for "their" tigers.

Now it's time to mention the more unpleasant parts of the

human-tiger relationship: exploitation and conflict.

If we could do it safely, many of us would enjoy touching a living tiger's fur, petting the cat and feeling its warmth and power.

But some people choose to take that fur, and other tiger body parts, for their own use. Many traditional Asian medicines have tiger ingredients, for example.

Despite protective legislation and international treaties, poaching is still a problem; as well, an estimated 6,000 tigers are "farmed" for this purpose. (*Goodrich et al.*)

There are also people who better appreciate this endangered cat but who wish that they didn't have to deal with it at work or near their homes.

Tiger attacks are a severe problem in some places.

In and around Nepal's Chitwan National Park, for example, 37 tigers killed 88 people between 1978 and 2006; there were 32 more deaths and 22 injuries between 2007 and 2014. (*Dhungana et al.*)

Tigers also killed about 40 people in the Sundarbans between 2000 and 2010 (*Goodrich et al.*) -- mostly honey collectors, fishermen, and wood gatherers. In Sumatra there were an estimated 8 deaths per year between 1978 and 1997. (*Das*)

Despite their size, tigers generally avoid us. The tragedies usually happen during an accidental encounter, but wild tigers occasionally do target human beings.

It's not easy to balance the needs of people and an endangered cat that's too large to fence in. Authorities do what they can to keep wild tigers and local people separate.

Red-list status

Endangered to Critically Endangered, depending on region.

The red-listing agency (IUCN, or the International Union

for the Conservation of Nature and Natural Resources)
https://www.iucnredlist.org/species/15955/50659951
and the Cat Specialist Group
http://www.catsg.org/index.php?id=124 offer detailed
information about tigers and the challenges facing those
who want to protect them.

Countries are taking action, too.

In 2010, Bangladesh, Bhutan, Cambodia, China, India,
Indonesia, Laos, Malaysia, Myanmar, Nepal, Russia,
Thailand, and Vietnam -- signed the St. Petersburg
declation (see hyperlink at chapter's end), agreeing to
stabilize and then double the number of wild tigers in the
world by 2022, the next Year of the Tiger.

While it remains to be seen whether the goal of increasing
global numbers to 6,000 tigers can be met, there is already
some good news.

India and Nepal already have met their national targets.

And in 2018, Russia's Amur Tiger Center estimated the current wild Amur/Siberian tiger population at 580 to 600.

Fossil relatives

All of us have at least one misconception about this.

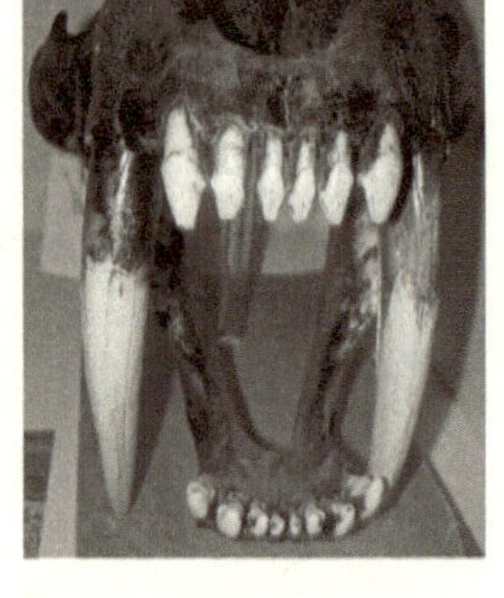

Let's set the record straight right now: There *never* was a sabertoothed tiger. Sabercats were members of the long extinct **Machairodontinae**, or "Knife-tooth" subfamily in Felidae.

Some of these cats were as big as today's tiger, or perhaps even bigger, but their upper canines were flat like, well, sabers. And their lower canines were unusually small (not that anyone ever said, "Gee, what unusually small lower canines!" when the living owner of those fossilized teeth, photographed by James St. John, CC BY 2.0, https://www.flickr.com/photos/jsjgeology/47626254461 , was coming after them).

And then there were conical-toothed cats, an entirely separate subfamily from the "Knife-tooths," sometimes called **Felinae**.

Tigers and the rest of today's cats are in this group, but none of them are, or ever were, "knife-tooths," i.e., sabertoothed cats. Both upper and lower canines are large and cone-shaped.

So, what real fossil relatives of the tiger have paleontologists unearthed?

Among the most notable finds are:

- *Panthera blytheae*. While there isn't a consensus yet about this four- to six-million-year-old cat, found in Tibet and reported by Tseng *et al.*, *P. blytheae* could be the ancestor of modern snow leopards and tigers, as well as the oldest known pantherine fossil cat!

- *Panthera palaeosinensis*. For a while, this two-million-year-old big cat from northern China was considered to be the oldest known fossil tiger. However, recent studies suggest that it may instead have been a member of one the mysterious "ghost lineages" taxonomists use to fill gaps between the fossil record and the age of a group shown by its DNA markers. For Panthera, that age is at least 10 million years (which is why experts are so excited about the much older *P. blytheae*).

- **The Longdan cat,** *Panthera zdanskyi.* In 2011, Mazák *et al.* described the beautifully preserved skull of a jaguar-sized big cat (found in Longdan, Gansu Province, China) that was built much more like a modern tiger than was *P. palaeosinensis.* And even better, at 2.55 to 2.16 million years old, it predates any other widely accepted tiger fossils! These researchers view the Longdan cat as a very primitive member of the feline branch that eventually led to tigers. Don't think too hard about how this relates to the other fossils mentioned here, though -- that gives even paleontologists a headache! Even with lots of fossils, it's difficult to reach a consensus on how everything fits together; with cats, there just isn't enough information available from the fossil record yet to do this. (*Johnson et al.; Werdelin et al.*)

- Chinese and Javan tigers. *P. palaeosinensis* and *P. zdanskyi* are very rare finds from the border time when Earth was in transition from its Pliocene epoch to the Pleistocene. Most tiger fossils are younger than this, "only" going back some 1.7 to 1.8 million years to the Middle to Late Pleistocene -- these are the fossil tigers of China and Java.

- Indian and Russian tigers: These ancient big cats only start to show up towards the end of the Pleistocene, some 12,000 years ago. Before rising seas drowned the Bering land bridge, tigers may also have made it to Alaska, where there was some open land in between two lobes of the great Laurentide continental ice sheet. If so, they didn't continue to spread across North America, as lions did. (*Kitchener and Yamaguchi*)

Life in the wild is never easy, and tigers seem to have had a challenging time of it during their time on Earth, particularly in the last 100,000 years or so.

It remains to be seen whether tigers will survive the existential crisis they're experiencing today. Perhaps they will, with a little help from their friends -- us.

Hyperlinks

- *Video*: Tiger chuffing.
  https://youtu.be/_UbDeqPdUek

- *Video*: Amur/Siberian tiger is released into wild:
  https://youtu.be/1dL81JPyFrY

- *Video*: Stalking tiger uses storm as cover:
  https://youtu.be/kK5Kq6tVMJg

- *Web page*: Messy Beast on domestic cat
  "brotherhoods": http://messybeast.com/soc_cat.htm

- *Video*: Tiger giving birth to two cubs:
  https://youtube.com/watch?v=SR6X-j55eEA

- *PDF download*: St. Petersburg declaration (English):
  http://cmsdata.iucn.org/downloads/st_petersburg_d
  eclaration_english.pdf

Melanistic leopard (black panther): John Shortland, CC BY.2.0
https://www.flickr.com/photos/16436271@N02/6159758831; Spotted leopard: Srikaanth Sekar, CC BY-SA 2.0,
https://www.flickr.com/photos/56017663@N03/9814267145

Leopards

Leopards have it all:

- That beautiful spotted or black coat ("black panthers" are melanistic leopards and quite common in parts of Southeast Asia)

- Big-cat power blended with the grace and agility of smaller cats

- Adaptability to a variety of different habitats and prey

So, why don't these predators own every ecosystem in
Asia and Africa?

Because pretty doesn't count in the wild. Size does
(though agility does, like tree-climbing skills that may save
a leopard's life, if not its dinner, when a lion moves in).

Leopards get pushed around a lot by their larger relatives.
But they hold on.

They even adjust to conditions that other big cats cannot
handle.

Such rugged flexibility is probably why a few populations
still inhabit much of the leopard's historic range
(*Uphyrkina et al.*), while lions and tigers have vanished
from much of theirs.

But only a few.

You see, leopards must also cope with *H. sapiens*. They're
still holding on, but it's not easy for them or for us.

Scientific name: *Panthera pardus*

There are leopard subspecies, too. The names vary by source.

That's not surprising, given how hard it is to study such a secretive wild cat and also considering how much the leopard's appearance changes over its vast range.

Amur leopard, by Tony Hisgett, CC BY 2.0 https://www.flickr.com/photos/hisgett/5017707785

Here's how two conservation groups -- the Cat Specialist Group and the International Union for Conservation of Nature (IUCN sets up the Red List) -- classify leopards at the time of writing:

Leopard subspecies

1. Amur and other leopards of Eastern Asia (*Panthera pardus orientalis*):   More information here. http://www.catsg.org/index.php?id=563 Critically Endangered.

2. Java leopard (*P. p. melas*): More information here. http://www.catsg.org/index.php?id=561 Critically Endangered.

3. Arabian leopard (*P. p. nimr*): More information here. http://www.catsg.org/index.php?id=560 Critically Endangered.

4. Persian leopard: I'm not sure of the scientific names. At the time of writing, IUCN calls the Persian leopard *P. p. saxicolor* and lists it as Endangered. However, the Cat Specialist Group includes this subspecies in *P. p. tulliana*, together with leopards in Turkey, the

Caucasus, Turkmenistan, Uzbekistan, Iran, Iraq, Afghanistan, and Pakistan, which are all listed as Vulnerable (a slightly lesser degree of extinction risk than "Endangered" but still worse than "Near Threatened").

5. Sri Lankan leopard (*P. p. kotiya*): More information here. http://www.catsg.org/index.php?id=562 Endangered.

6. African leopard (*P. p. pardus*): Vulnerable.

7. Indian leopard (*P. p. fusca*): More information here. http://www.catsg.org/index.php?id=584 Vulnerable.

8. Indochinese leopard (*P. p. delacouri*): This is the IUCN's term for leopards found in Southeast Asia and probably southern China. Vulnerable.

Data

These are from the Cat Specialist Group unless otherwise noted. (Image of Javan leopard by Tambako the Jaguar, CC BY-ND 2.0,

https://www.flickr.com/photos/tambako/27660903149)

- Weight: 40 to 200 pounds. That's not a typo.
  Animals adapt to various climates and habitats is by
  altering their body mass. The size of available prey
  matters, too. The largest leopards are found in Africa
  -- home to the only megafauna that survived the end-
  Pleistocene extinctions. Leopards in the mountains
  of Iran and Central Asia are also quite hefty.   Another
  factor is the size difference between genders; it's
  there in all cats, but male leopards can be so much
  larger that some old-time naturalists mistook them
  for a separate species! (*Sunquist and Sunquist*) That
  said, you don't typically see 40-pound females and
  200-pound males of the same subspecies.

- Body length: 36 to 75 inches.

- Tail length: 20 to 40 inches.

- Coat: The idea that leopards are spotted *golden* cats
  is really more of a suggestion than a rule. Some are

orange, grayish yellow, or even buff gray! Those living near the Equator have more intense fur color. Something about the humid tropical forests, particularly on Java and in peninsular Malaysia, seems to encourage melanism. In the cool north, Amur leopards are light in color and shaggy, especially during winter. African leopards on the savannah have reddish to ocher background fur, while those in drier parts of Africa are more tawny. Every leopard's coat also shows black/brown spots and rosettes, which are spots arranged in larger circles or squares that usually with a light-colored center. Spots may show up anywhere, but rosettes usually appear on the cat's back and flanks. Individual leopards can be identified by these markings and other coat characteristics. All fur on the underparts is typically white. A leopard's tail has a mix of spots, blobs, rings and other dark marks -- the extreme tip is black on the outer part and white on the inside portion. Fur behind the ear is white (upper half) and black (lower half). (*Cat Specialist Group; Heptner and Sludskii; Sunquist and Sunquist; Uphyrkina et al.*)

- Vocals: The leopard's signature sound is "sawing", though it's labeled a roar in many online videos. Whatever you choose to call it, this remarkable sound carries up to 2 miles through the still air during mating season. I couldn't find any authoritative mention of a leopard roar, but they do grunt, mew, snarl, spit, and hiss. Leopards also apparently "puff," but that's described as more like a lion's sociable greeting than the friendly "chuff" of tigers and a few other big cats. (*Ewer; Sunquist and Sunquist*)

- Average litter size: 1-4 cubs; per Ewer, usually 2-3.

- Life span: 13 to 21 years.

Arabian leopard by Land Rover Our Planet, BY-ND 2.0 https://www.flickr.com/photos/our-planet/5764223665

Features unique to leopards

The famous spotted coat? Not so much, actually.

As we'll see in the next chapter, the New World's only big cat also sports that look.

But *P. pardus* is absolutely unique in other ways:

- Leopards have the **greatest geographic range of any cat** (you might already suspect this after meeting subspecies that range from the Russian Far East down to Java and Africa). During the ice ages and into Neolithic times, leopards also roamed western and central Europe.

- Of all Old World cats, the leopard can handle the **widest range of habitats** -- basically anything between the sea and timberline, except a true desert like the Sahara. To the consternation of local citizens, leopards have even established themselves in urban areas, including the outskirts of Mumbai and Johannesburg, so skillfully that people seldom realize they are there.

- Leopards have the broadest diet of any large hypercarnivore (not just cats). (*Jacobson et al.*) They'll eat anything from insects to ibexes. Some Indian leopards have been observed chowing down on watermelons! (*Sunquist and Sunquist*)

- This is also the largest spotted cat in Asia and Africa.

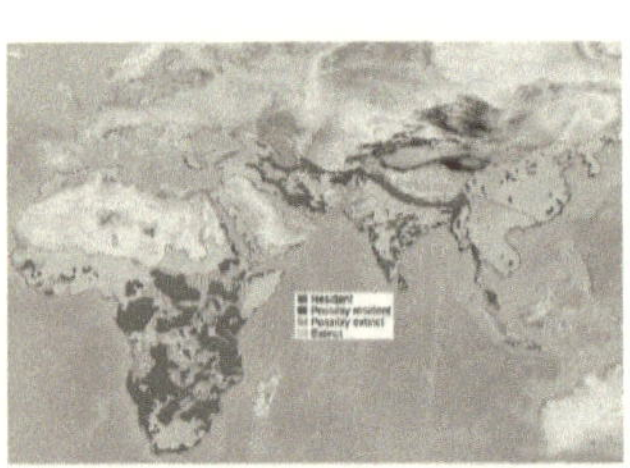

Where found in the wild

Given its adaptability, *P. pardus* can turn up wherever there is at least a little cover, as this map by BhagyaMani via Wikimedia https://en.wikipedia.org/wiki/Leopard#/media/File:Leopard_distribution.jpg, shows. The only factors limiting leopards seem to be the presence of people (though they do generally try to avoid us) and competition from other predators.

Today's leopard country runs from the Russian Far East down through subtropical and tropical Asia, including the island of Java (but not Borneo or Sumatra, for some reason); westward across India into the Middle East; and southward into sub-Saharan Africa.

In southwestern and central Asia, leopards are sighted mainly in the more remote mountains and rugged foothill areas. They have been observed at elevations up to 17,000 feet in the Himalayas.

Amur leopards -- like this one photographed by Alexander Leisser, CC BY-SA 4.0, via Wikimedia https://commons.wikimedia.org/wiki/File:Amurleopard_(Panthera_pardus)_im_Schnee.jpg -- can handle subzero temps for weeks at a time during wintertime but probably not deep snow.

Africa has the most leopards today, generally in grasslands, open woods, and forested environments. They don't always have an easy time of it -- on the Serengeti, lions chase them on sight!

These leopards keep close to thickets and riverine forests, leaving the open areas to the prides. (*Seidensticker et al.*)

In terms of geographic area, the leopard's range is the same as it was in the mid-18th century. However, cats only cover about a third of it, because of human activities. (*Jacobson et al.*)

It's the usual sad story that has played out for pantherines over the last couple of centuries - hunting, retaliation killing, loss of prey, and fragmentation or destruction of habitat as cities, settlements, and agricultural lands expand into the wild. (See links in the Red List section farther down for more details.)

Leopards can cope with these changes better than most other big cats, but even they have taken some hard hits down through the years.

Closest cat family relatives

Panthera is the oldest branch on the cat family tree. In this sense, there's some distance between any big cat and other feline lineages.

Molecular markers show that all pantherines have a common ancestor (which hasn't been found yet in the fossil record).

Overall, these studies of big-cat DNA suggest that leopards, lions, and jaguars might be a little more closely related to one another than to tigers or snow leopards.

Experts disagree on the precise connections among these three feline species, though.

Some -- for instance, Johnson *et al.* -- interpret the results as showing that jaguars are genetically a little closer to lions than leopards are; others, like Davis *et al.*, find that leopards and lions group together, with the jaguar on the sidelines this time.

This is one of those esoteric scientific debates that probably won't be settled until more fossil cats are dug out of the ground.

Famous leopards

- There are many legends about "panthers" and "pards" that usually, but not always, involve a spotted big cat. It's not always clear if that's truly a leopard, though.

- And then there's Mowgli's protector **Bagheera**, a "black panther" in *The Jungle Book*.

- The most famous real-life leopard is **Nissa**, Hollywood actor during the mid-20th century.

How leopards hunt and live

Stealthy, bold, and versatile -- this description by Sunquist and Sunquist fits the leopard very well.

Until the arrival of digital cameras, very few people had ever observed a leopard hunt. That's a testimony to the leopard's elusiveness as well as the ruggedness of the terrain it often is found in.

As widespread as leopards are, there is surprisingly little detailed information on their life in the wild.

We do know that, in open habitats like Africa's woodlands,

leopards not only use trees as escape routes and for
resting but also as vantage points to spot prey for stalking.

And also for just hanging out. (Flowcomm CC BY 2.0 https://www.flickr.com/photos/flowcomm/11665212566/)

Hauling a carcass into a tree is something leopards do
more often in Africa; in Asia, they use dense cover for
caching. (*Sunquist and Sunquist*)

When it comes to stalking, eyewitnesses have reported
leopards using almost anything, including vehicles and
even a dust devil, as cover.

In forests, they may instead wait patient in ambush near fruit-bearing vegetation or a heavily used game trail.

On the ground or in trees, leopards will take anything from a bird or little rock hyrax to a one-ton eland.

In general, per the Cat Specialist Group:

The leopard has an exceptional ability to adapt to changes in prey availability. However, the leopard prefers medium sized ungulates [hoofed animals] with a weight of 10-40 kg [22-88 pounds] but can kill prey up to 2 to 3 times larger than itself.

Individuals sometimes show food preferences, particularly for canids like jackals and domestic dogs. Some even specialize in porcupines!

Leopards do deserve their killer reputation, but they must work hard to earn it. Sunquist and Sunquist report that their overall success rate might not be very high.

However, these hypercarnivores are well adapted to a feast/famine diet.

After surviving on anything they can get, leopards will
eventually gorge themselves on a sizable kill, eating up to
a quarter of their own body weight at a time.

How leopards reproduce

Big cat females act just like
house cats do when they're
in heat. This lonely lady
lives in a Swiss zoo (image:
Tambako the Jaguar, CC
BY-ND 2.0,

https://www.flickr.com/photos/tambako/4706457301).

But very little is known about leopard life in the wild. This
information, from the Cat Specialist Group, Ewer, and
Sunquist and Sunquist, is mostly from those observed in
zoos or on protected reserves:

- Gestation: 90-95 days. Mating and births can be in
  any season.

- Birth weight: 1 to 2 pounds.

- Eyes open at 6 to 9 days. These two cubs, Satka and Liski, probably aren't much older than that (image: Tambako the Jaguar, CC BY-ND 2.0, https://www.flickr.com/photos/tambako/15575016840)

- The cubs begin to take meat at around 40 days and are weaned at about 12 weeks. Around that time, they weigh 7 to 9 pounds and often start travelling together.

- Permanent canines come in at around 8 months.

- It takes time to learn the survival skills these young pantherines will need. That's why youngsters usually stay with Mom for 12 to 18 months before going out on their own.

Of note, the gene that causes melanism in leopards is recessive. In plain English (and per those rules of Mendelian inheritance you might remember from grade school), this means that spotted and black leopard cubs can appear in the same litter.

If there are many "black panthers" around -- on the Malay Peninsula, for example, where it's rare to see a spotted leopard -- most cubs will be black, too, since it's more likely that both parents carry the gene mutation.

Interactions with people

Relax. Fashions like this became unacceptable in the West before the turn of the century. (Image: Libricool via Wikimedia, public domain,

https://upload.wikimedia.org/wikipedia/commons/a/a9/Leopard_fur_skin_coat.jpg)

Still, it's a good thing for us that leopards don't hold grudges.

A little fear of leopards is not unreasonable.

Of all endangered cats, they're the most suited for getting a little of their own back -- they can tolerate human presence.

More than any other big cat, leopards are comfortable living around people, even in urban areas. While they generally keep a very low profile, this is not good news for anyone involved.

When a leopard is discovered in town, even if it hasn't done any harm, things get just as crazy as you would expect.

Animal Rescue India made this video of an urban leopard being captured: https://youtu.be/aCK_-UU78K0

They report that, despite struggling and some attacks from a mob of local citizens, the leopard sustained only minor injuries during its capture and was released later in an area deemed safe for everyone involved.

Global statistics show that tigers and lions are more likely to attack humans, but when a leopard does turn to man-eating, it's bad.

Since leopards are able to tolerate our world, a man-eater can slink around our infrastructure undetected. There are confirmed reports of leopards entering buildings, breaking through doors and windows if need be.

Most home invasions, though, are accidental, as with this leopard that charged in while chasing the family dog: https://www.upi.com/Odd_News/2019/11/25/Home-invading-leopard-captured-in-India/1081574702865/

If you checked that link out, you could see from looking at its posture that the leopard deeply regrets its move but doesn't know what to do next. Fortunately for all concerned, people in the house did.

Everyone kept their cool. Animal control was called, and

they captured the big cat unharmed, later releasing it back into the wild farther away from people.

Unfortunately, not everyone handles these unexpected encounters as well -- tragedies do happen.

India has the highest number of human-leopard conflicts. There, between 1999 and 2005, 902 people were injured and 201 died. (*Athreya et al.*)

One of the most difficult challenges in felid conservation is finding a way for people to coexist with wild leopards (especially in India), while at the same time conserving as many of these beautiful cats as we possibly can.

Red-listed?

Taking a leopard census in the wild is impossible for many reasons, not least because of the wide geographic area where this cat is found and its skill in avoiding researchers.

The boffins do the best they can. As more and more information has come in since the 1980s, the leopard's conservation status has varied from Vulnerable to Least Concern back to Vulnerable again, where it has remained since 2015, with the exceptions as noted above for subspecies.

Check out felid conservation websites, like the Cat Specialist Group http://www.catsg.org/index.php?id=110 , the IUCN https://www.iucnredlist.org/species/15954/102421779 , and Panthera https://www.panthera.org/cat/leopard , for the latest information.

Fossil relatives

Palaeontologists report that a leopard-sized big cat lived in what is now Tanzania some three to four million years ago. They do tentatively link it with *P. pardus*, but its precise relationship to modern leopards or other pantherines is still under debate. (*Werdelin and Dehghani*)

The oldest unequivocal leopard fossils are about two

million years old and also come from Africa. About a million years after those African cats lived, leopards were prowling across much of Eurasia. (*Werdelin et al.*)

They don't seem to have crossed into the Americas, though. However, there is a very leopard-like big cat in the New World today . . .

- *Video*: Lion steals leopard's dinner: https://youtu.be/v4KACj6ErgY

- *Video*: Leopard "sawing": https://youtu.be/oZigyLQeAQw

- *Video*: Leopard stalking impala in gully: https://youtu.be/LhSDxp0oQK8

- *Video*: Leopard hunting in trees: https://youtu.be/R51orTJkgj4

- *Web page*: Nissa, the Hollywood leopard: http://animal-actors.blogspot.com/2010/01/nissa-aka-baby.html

- *Video*: Karula, a game-reserve African leopard, and her two cubs: https://youtu.be/A-20asCKA_s

Jaguars

For thousands of years, people have had the highest regard for jaguars, which resemble leopards but are much more powerfully built.

Peru's Chavin culture, for example, made jaguar sculptures.

Later, the Olmec people spoke in hushed tones of were-jaguars, while others, including the Maya, used the jaguar as a symbol of political and military power.

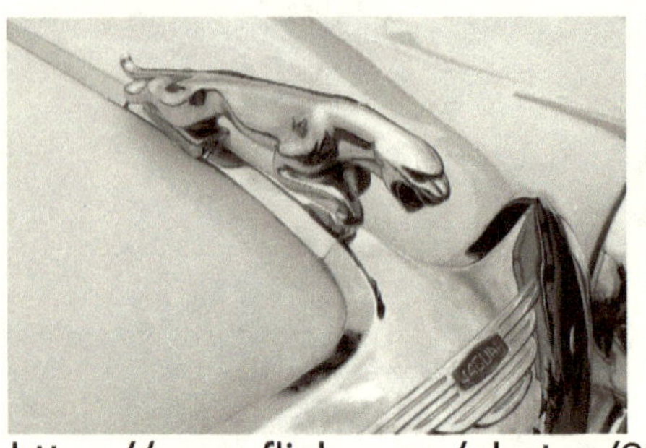

We moderns aren't immune to the jaguar's fascination, either, as this image by John Lloyd, CC BY 2.0, https://www.flickr.com/photos/32109282@N00/4827636 3132, shows.

What many of us might not realize, though, is that the jaguar is right up there with lions, tigers, and leopards in the Panthera lineage. It's also the only big cat that's native to the Americas.

Scientific name: *Panthera onca.*

Genetic testing shows four distinct jaguar populations:

1. Mexico and Guatemala

2. Southern Central America

3. South America, north of the Amazon River

<ol start="4">
<li>South America, south of the Amazon</li>
</ol>

However, this doesn't necessarily translate into jaguar subspecies. That's a very controversial issue just now.

You will see subspecies listed in online sources, like Wikipedia. However, the Cat Specialist Group and several other sources presently use just the one species name -- *P. onca* -- though this could change in the future.

Data

These are from the Cat Specialist Group (CSG) website unless otherwise noted.

- **Weight:** 80 to a little over 300 pounds.   As with the leopard, this is not a typo. While most jaguars look like this one (image

by Eddy Van 3000, CC BY-SA 2.0,
https://www.flickr.com/photos/e3000/5486315005),
Sunquist and Sunquist say that there is no such thing
as an "average" jaguar in terms of size. This seems to
be more about location than gender (though male
jaguars are usually larger than females in any given
place). The biggest jaguars live near the Equator;
body size gradually decreases as *P. onca* ranges
farther north and south. Jaguars in Brazil's Pantanal,
for instance, weigh at least 160 to 225 pounds, while
in parts of Central America, some don't even reach the
100-pound mark. (*CSG; Sunquist and Sunquist;
Turner and Antón*)

- Body length: 43 to 67 inches.

- Tail length: 17 to 32 inches.

- Coat: Background fur color is pale yellow to tawny
  brown, with spotted white fur on the cat's underparts.
  Black jaguars are relatively common, just as with
  leopards; however, it's from a different gene mutation.
  (*Eizirik et al., 2003; Kitchener et al., 2010*). The

jaguar's coat spots and rosettes are very similar, though no one knows why. One way to tell them apart is by looking for a small spot inside a rosette (that larger square or circle made up of small spots) -- jaguars usually have this, leopards almost never do. Also, fur on the back of a jaguar's ear is typically black, with a faint spot; with leopards, there is a more distinctive white/black marking.

- Vocals: Besides making typical feline noises like mewing (*Wikipedia*), jaguars "chuff" among friends and family, as do tigers, snow leopards, and clouded leopards. They do not purr. The jaguar's roar is sometimes compared to thunder. However, the online videos I checked mostly showed jaguars "sawing" like a leopard. The San Diego Zoo's online jaguar page describes a male's roar as "more like a bark, followed by a growl," while the female's is "a sound like a coughing roar." Sunquist and Sunquist report that as many as four jaguars at a time have been heard calling back and forth. Imagine hearing that in the Amazon rainforest or on some Latin American hillside!

- Average litter size: 1 to 4 cubs, usually 2 (*Sunquist and Sunquist*)

- Average life span: Up to 26 years, per the Cat Specialist Group. This is probably in captivity, where jaguars thrive (many wild cats don't); longevity in the wild isn't well known, per Sunquist and Sunquist.

Features unique to this cat

- Besides being the only big cat in the Americas, jaguars are also the **largest Latin American carnivore.** (*Sunquist and Sunquist*)

- Jaguars are the heaviest cat that routinely climbs. Sure, you'll see videos and pictures of lions in a tree, but they never seem very comfortable. Jaguars can hunt just as well in trees as on the ground!

- Turner and Antón -- experts in feline anatomy -- write that modern jaguars may have the most robust build of ALL known cats, living and extinct, including every sabercat except Smilodon and a few species of Megantereon (Smilodon's ancestor).

- Too, jaguars have a more powerful jaw than any other big cat. (*Cat Specialist Group; Quigley et al.*) How powerful? Here's a video of a jaguar using its jaws to pierce the armored braincase of a caiman (a crocodile relative) and then to carry the heavy carcass off: https://youtu.be/DBNYwxDZ_pA .

- This is the only big cat to regularly kill prey with a skull bite. (*Cat Specialist Group*) Like other cats, jaguars also dispatch prey with either a bite to the back of the neck for smaller animals or a suffocating throat bite for big ones.

Where found in the wild

Historically, jaguars have ranged from the US states of Washington and Oregon south to Patagonia, at the tip of South America. (*Eizirik et al., 2001; Sunquist and Sunquist*)

Today, a few are still seen in the Southwest, mainly Arizona. (*Cat Specialist Group*)

Here, almost invisible in the grass, is a jaguar wandering through Arizona's Santa Rita Mountains, camera-trapped in 2012 by the US Fish and Wildlife Service, public domain, https://www.flickr.com/photos/usfws_southwest/8291363911.

However, most jaguars live in Mexico, Central America, and South America down to the Rio Negro in Argentina -- a little over half their historic range.

Their main stronghold is in Amazonia. That makes sense. Jaguars prefer dense cover, but it isn't very high (generally at elevations below 3000 feet, although a few jaguars have been observed up to about 10,000 feet).

(Image: Land Rover Our Planet: Jaguar in Atlantic Forest, CC BY-ND 2.0 https://www.flickr.com/photos/our-planet/5909901664)

This jaguar is in Brazil's Atlantic coast rainforest, but the big cats are found in other environments, too. As long as there's enough water and sufficient prey, jaguars are quite happy in a variety of habitats, even dry thornscrub and lowland pasture land!

Closest cat family relatives

There isn't a consensus yet on just exactly how lions, leopards, and jaguars are related, but almost everyone

agrees that these three pantherines have more in common
with one another than with snow leopards or tigers.

That may seem strange, since jaguars and leopards today
occupy two very different parts of the world, but their
ancestors and those of the lion did mingle back in the day.

Lions did reach the Americas during the ice ages. Too, the
fossil record does contain a European jaguar, as we'll see
a little farther down in this chapter.

How jaguars hunt and live

Leopards -- the jaguar's apparent twin -- are limited to
some extent by lions or tigers, but not jaguars.

Jaguars have been New World apex predators ever since
sabercats went extinct at the end of the last ice age.
(*Smith et al.*)

They may be active either by day or during the night. It

depends on what their prey does and perhaps also on whether there are any human disturbances in the area. (*Sunquist and Sunquist*).

This female jaguar, photographed by Tambako the Jaguar, CC BY-ND 2.0,

https://www.flickr.com/photos/tambako/8074740407, is hunting capybara rodents.

If there's enough cover nearby, jaguars may go into open areas, but they prefer thick overgrowth and typically hunt by walking slowly along trails or beaches, watching and listening for prey.

The jaguar is a ground hunter, although it's also an excellent swimmer and very agile in the trees. However, it's not built for high-speed pursuit.

Typically, jaguars wait in ambush or get as close to prey as possible before charging.

More than 85 prey species have been identified, but peccaries and other ungulates (hoofed mammals) are often taken, as are turtles in some parts of South America (jaguars can get into the shell and sometimes eat small turtles whole).

However, like leopards, jaguars aren't fussy when it comes to food. As generalists, they will eat almost anything, from turtle eggs up to thousand-pound cows.

Ewer reports that some jaguars even like avocados! This captive jaguar is enjoying a tasty veggie treat! (Image: C. Watts, CC BY 2.0, https://www.flickr.com/photos/watts_photos/250294487 62/)

Jaguars will usually drag a kill into dense cover before

starting to feed. They've been observed hauling large carcasses a mile or more, sometimes over rugged terrain.

That takes some strength!

How jaguars reproduce

The path of love is often rocky when it involves two apex predators (this courting pair were photographed in the Pantanal by Bernie Dupont, CC BY-SA 2.0, https://flickr.com/photos/65695019@N07/27908098425).

Not much is known about wild jaguar family life, though cubs apparently are born any time of year near the Equator; there seems to be more seasonality in jaguar breeding farther north and south.

In captivity, woolly spotted cubs are born after a three- to four-month gestation. They typically weigh 1-1/2 to 2 pounds each.

The cubs' eyes open during the first two weeks of life, and they'll put on almost 6 pounds over the next seven weeks.

By age three months, jaguar cubs are large enough to accompany Mom to kills. They can take some meat now but continue suckling for another couple of months.

By six months of age, the youngsters are on a hypercarnivorous diet. They're not ready for life on their own yet, though.

As with other cats, predator training school takes some time -- generally two to four years.

As with most cats, when they reach maturity females will probably settle down near Mom, as long as there is enough prey in the area to support everybody, while young males go off to get territories farther away.

Interactions with people

As we've seen, jaguar imagery played a big role in early Mesoamerican culture. This image of a jaguar warrior, for instance (via Wikimedia

https://commons.wikimedia.org/wiki/File:Tovar_Codex_(f

olio_134).png), is from one of the Aztec codices.

Today, traditional jaguar dances are popular in parts of Mexico (and probably elsewhere). But the story told by this "Danza de los Tecuanes" is a little sad from a cat lover's perspective.

In brief, the jaguar is seemingly invincible, but the hunters eventually kill it, and everybody celebrates.

The historical reality is the sad part. Jaguars once were numerous in Mexico and still are found in some areas, but they have been extirpated from many parts of the country.

It's not the folk dancers' fault, of course. They are celebrating their heritage.

Rather, there are complex reasons for the decline in jaguar numbers.

- They were hit hard by the fur trade until public opinion in many countries turned against this fashion.

- Jaguar habitat has been broken up or degraded as people developed the land.

- Hunters take the same game animals that these big cats depend on for food.

- Many big cattle ranches in South America are in prime jaguar territory. The big cats sometimes prey on those domestic herds, leading to retaliation and persecution.

Prime jaguar country in Brazil -- you can see the potential for human-jaguar conflict here. (Image: Ronaldo Almeida/Shutterstock)

However, in addition to retaliation for predation on livestock, Cavalcanti *et al.* report that, at least in Brazil, there is still a culture of celebrating the killing of a jaguar.

Are jaguars dangerous to people?

Any cat that size is, of course. But, unlike leopards, jaguars try hard to avoid us.

So seldom do they attack people that an unprovoked attack on a sleeping Brazilian fisherman in 2008 made national headlines.

Red-listed?

Yes, as Near Threatened. **More** information: https://www.iucnredlist.org/species/15953/123791436

Jaguars have disappeared from about half of their historic range, but their conservation picture is better than that of the other big cats.

Jaguars with the best outlook are those inhabiting parts of Colombia and Central America, as well as in the Amazon rainforest and adjacent areas, such as Brazil's Pantanal and Gran Chaco.

This region encompasses about 70% of the cat's present range.

Jaguar populations elsewhere are more isolated and therefore at higher risk of extinction.

To improve their chances, for survival, wildlife biologists are building a network of wildlife corridors like those in southern Asia that, per Thapa *et al.*, may already be helping tiger numbers increase.

Fossil relatives

Many experts think that modern jaguars are related to a much larger fossil cat -- the European jaguar, a/k/a *Panthera gombaszoegensis*.

European and American fossil jaguars were much larger than modern jaguars like this one (image: Tambako the Jaguar, CC BY-ND 2.0, https://www.flickr.com/photos/tambako/30762209384).

The Early to Middle Pleistocene European jaguar may have weighed over 400 pounds!

Its fossils were first identified in Slovakia during the 1930s, and other forms have been found in Italy, France, and the Netherlands. (*Wikipedia*)

Jaguars in the Americas also go back to the earliest Pleistocene, some 1.5 million years ago. These big cats tended to be more numerous in places where there weren't many American lions (*Panthera atrox*), for example, what are now the states of Florida, Texas, and Tennessee. (*Turner and Antón*)

The best known fossil jaguars in the New World are *P. onca augusta*, or North American jaguar, and *P. onca mesembrina*, in South America. There are also unidentified jaguar fossils on both continents.

The overall picture appears to be one in which North American jaguars vanished, along with many other species, in the end-Pleistocene extinctions, while *P. onca mesembrina* evolved into the modern jaguar.

But much more needs to be learned about jaguar history and evolution.

Meanwhile, let's return to the Old World and meet two other big cats. Each has the word "leopard" in its name, but one lives at high altitudes while the other prefers humid equatorial rainforests.

- *Video*: Jaguars chuffing:
  https://youtu.be/nDm1pG0LNzc

- *Web page*: San Diego Zoo jaguar page:
  https://animals.sandiegozoo.org/animals/jaguar

- *Video*: Jaguar catching a monkey in tree-top chase:
  https://youtu.be/mD9081S7oCg

- *Video*: Danza de los Tecuanes (Spanish):
  https://youtu.be/ZvnGdmB0PkU

Snow leopard

Until recently, this beautiful feline resident of the world's highest mountain ranges sorely puzzled experts.

Snow leopards are rare; they also live in remote places that, in addition to being extremely rugged, are sometimes political hot spots and/or war zones.

All this kept researchers from studying them in detail until the 1970s -- two centuries after the species was first described by Western naturalists.

What little was known about snow leopards only added to their mystery.

- Though they're the size of a small leopard and don't purr, snow leopards have never been heard to roar. This raised the question, how could they be one of the "roaring cats" (the original definition of big cats)?

- You can't see it under all that fur, but the snow leopard's long legs and tail, and its small, rounded head, resemble those of the cheetah. Since neither cat is what you might call a typical member of family Felidae, could this mean that snow leopards and cheetahs are related?

Unable to reach a consensus, early 20th-century zoologists simply gave snow leopards their own category -- Uncia, a word derived from a common term for spotted wild cats -- and waited for more information to come along.

Scientific name: *Panthera uncia*.

This used to be *Uncia uncia*.

*"Whatever."--Snow leopard. (Image: Tambako the Jaguar, CC BY-ND 2.0,
https://www.flickr.com/photos/tambako/47380023111)*

When DNA testing became a thing, zoologists were able to
solve the puzzle. It turned out that snow leopards are very
closely related genetically to *tigers*, not cheetahs
(*Johnson et al.; Kitchener et al., 2017; Nyakatura and
Bininda-Emonds*).

Not everyone agrees with that (see Christiansen). Still, it does prove snow leopards are big cats (and, incidentally, that roaring isn't a necessary qualification for membership in this ancient lineage, to which snow leopards were added in 2008).

And those long legs and the snow leopard's domed skull?

They're adaptations similar to the cheetah's (which is large, but not a pantherine).

It's all about lifestyle. Cheetahs need speed and balance on the plains. Snow leopards use *their* long legs and tail to chase nimble prey across almost vertical rocky cliffs.

As for the skull, doming widens the nasal passages, and both these cats need lots of air!

Cheetahs basically need to air-cool their brain after working so hard during a chase across the hot plains.

Snow leopards live at high altitudes and must take in more air just to get enough oxygen to live and hunt.

Data

These are from the Cat Specialist Group website unless otherwise noted.

- Weight: 66 to 110 pounds.

- Height at the shoulder: 24 inches. (*Jackson et al.*)

- Body length: 35 to 47 inches.

- Tail length: 32 to 39 inches. Besides providing balance during cliff-edge acrobatics, a "supertail" with fluffy fur that makes it as thick as a human arm also makes a warm wrap-around

when the cat is lying down or sitting. (Image: Eric Kilby, CC BY-SA 2.0, https://www.flickr.com/photos/ekilby/13883254224)

- Coat: Individual snow leopards can be identified by their markings, which include rosettes like those of a leopard, plus black spots over the head, neck, and legs -- this is all on a much paler background fur color, though. Two dark lines also typically extend from the cat's neck to its tail. Overall, these colors and patterning provide such good camouflage that snow leopards are almost impossible to see when they're in amongst rocks or patchy snow. They also have thick cushions of fur on their massive paws, perhaps for insulation as well as for "snowshoeing" like a lynx. (*Cat Specialist Group; Jackson et al.; Sunquist and Sunquist; Turner and Antón*)

- Vocals: Anatomy studies show the ability to roar or to purr depends on the vocal folds, not the hyoid bone structure in the throat as was previously suspected. Snow leopards lack the right vocal fold qualities to produce either a roar or a purr. This doesn't stop them from making other common feline sounds.

Snow leopards also produce a loud yowl during mating season that can be heard above the noise of a fast-moving mountain river and over long distances. Too, they chuff in friendly situations or for reassurance, as do tigers, leopards, and jaguars. (*Cat Specialist Group; Christiansen; Kitchener et al., 2010; Sunquist and Sunquist*)

* Average litter size: 1-5 (typically 2, per Ewer).

* Average life span: 10 to 20 years. Presumably that is for captives; Jackson *et al.* note that there is no information on snow leopard longevity in the wild.

Features unique to this cat

- While Amur leopards and tigers can be pretty shaggy, snow leopards have the longest, densest fur of any big cat -- up to 5 inches long in wintertime, and with some 4,000 guard hairs per square centimeter. (*Cat Specialist Group; Kitchener et al., 2010; Heptner and Sludskii*)

- We've mentioned some of the physical changes snow

leopards have evolved for life in the mountains. They also are the only cat species with genetic adaptations similar to those found in people who live at high altitude (namely, per Wang *et al.*, unique amino acid changes related to factors that increase the number of red blood cells as well as the amount of oxygen-carrying hemoglobin in the blood).

- Sunquist and Sunquist report that snow leopards eat vegetation more frequently than any other cat. All cats are hypercarnivores, meaning that they must eat meat, but many of them do occasionally go for greens and no one really knows why. It might be to rid themselves of intestinal parasites. In the snow leopard's case, given its extreme environment, perhaps plants somehow supplement their diet nutritionally and/or filling in during the famine that comes to most wild cats in between the occasional feast.

Where found in the wild

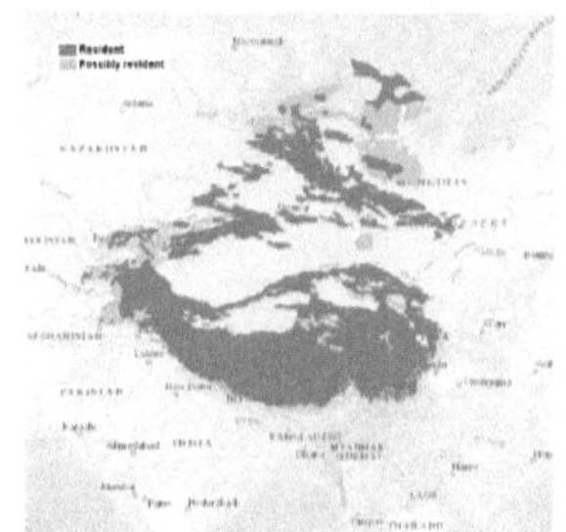

As this image by BhagyaMani via

Wikimedia, CC BY-SA 4.0, https://commons.wikimedia.org/wiki/File:SnowLeopard_distribution.jpg shows, snow leopard country includes (per the Cat Specialist Group):

- Russia's Altai mountains; here, at the northern limit of their range, the cats generally stay below 10,000 feet, sometimes as low as 1600 feet.

- The Tian Shan and Kun Lun ranges

- Central Asia's Pamir Mountains

- The Hindu Kush

- The Karakorum Mountains bordering India, Pakistan, Afghanistan, and China

- The Himalayas

These big cats have been observed as high as 18,000 feet in the Himalayas, but they're generally found between about 9800 to 16,400 feet.

Life in such harsh places has no frills -- snow leopards live wherever they

can find prey. (*McCarthy et al.*)

This is mainly medium-sized hoofed animals like wild sheep and goats, (though snow leopards will take marmots and other small prey now and then).

And as this image by Adam Greig CC BY-SA 2.0, https://www.flickr.com/photos/randomskk/25229325200 /, shows, blue sheep and other snow leopard prey, are hard-core, too.

During summer, snow leopards hang out above timberline, where sheep, goats, and other tasty herbivores are grazing across small plateaus or gentle slopes covered in alpine vegetation, as well as in narrow valleys and along the walls of rocky gorges carved by rushing streams and rivers.

As winter approaches, snow leopards follow their migrating meals down to the tree-shrub zone. Winter finds them even farther down the mountainside, stalking prey through open conifer forests.

Heptner and Sludskii see snow leopards as both alpine predators and rock specialists.

In such terrain, the big cats can cross cliffs and travel along stony ridges that wind has cleared of snow. Besides freedom of movement, rocks also provide good cover, especially in treeless areas.

Closest cat family relatives

Most, though not all, experts agree that molecular studies show a very close link between snow leopards and tigers. However, the relationship between these two pantherines and the rest of the big cats is still under debate. (*Christiansen; Werdelin et al.*)

How snow leopards hunt and live

Blue sheep and Siberian ibexes are at the top of the menu -- one snow leopard can take 20 to 30 of them each year. (*Macdonald et al., 2010*)

The cats usually move along straight features in the landscape, like ridges or the base of a cliff.

During the day they rest, either concealed by rocks and vegetation (if any is present) or sunning themselves on a ledge. Snow leopards are most active at dusk and at dawn.

Targets are typically medium in size, but snow leopards can handle larger animals, too. They stalk from above and then come crashing down on their victim, chasing it down the cliff like this: https://youtu.be/Uj0EVT-Ekog

If not disturbed, snow leopards stay with the kill rather than hiding the carcass or returning just to feed. However, they quickly flee without fighting for the meal when any sort of threat approaches.

Snow leopards set up typical feline territories, with the males basing theirs on the presence of females and the she-cats basing theirs on food resources.

And just like other kitties, snow leopards patrol these territories, pausing now and then to leave a scent mark on the local social media "page" a lot like Fluffy does at home.

Cats never tell us the meaning of their messages, but the scent marking shown in that video may be a time-sharing note rather than "No Trespassing!" or a sexy come-on.

There isn't much available real estate up here, so multiple cats may use the same core area, each one occupying it at a different time. (*Jackson et al.*)

How snow leopards reproduce

"Mom? Mom? Mom! Mom?! Mom!!" (Image: Eric Kilby, CC BY-SA 2.0,

https://www.flickr.com/photos/ekilby/29231043317)

The snow leopard's mating calls echo through the rocky heights from early January to mid-March. Most cubs are born in spring and early summer -- the most forgiving season in snow leopard country.

These fuzzy newborns weigh almost a pound to a pound and a half. Their blue eyes taken seven or eight days to open and gradually acquire the adult eye color -- gray or green -- as the weeks pass.

The cubs put on almost a pound a week while nursing and

are ready for their first taste of meat at a month or so.

At around 3 months old, they're completely weaned but still have much to learn.

Snow leopard behavior in the wild isn't very well understood yet, but frisky cubs may start accompanying Mom on hunts at some point between ages 2 and 4 months.

However, young snow leopards won't be fully prepared to survive until a year and a half to two years have passed.

Even after they eventually leave home, siblings will sometimes stay together for a few more months before finally embarking on their individual lives as a solitary apex predator.

Interactions with people

Snow leopards are fairly easy-going, for big cats, and some of them even have been tamed.

However, conflict is still a problem, and not just with livestock owners.

"Artillery? Firefights? Up here?" -- Snow leopard. (Image: Haseebamjad88 via Wikimedia, CC BY-SA 3.0 https://commons.wikimedia.org/wiki/File:The_Snow_Leopard.jpg)

1. **Human-human conflict.** Wars and lesser-scale troubles have happened with depressing regularity in snow leopard country during the last half-century or so. As well, about a third of the cat's range includes political hot spots and disputed borders. This makes it very difficult to set up international protocols and other agreements to protect snow leopards, even when bullets and missiles aren't flying around.

2. **Human-snow leopard conflict.** Few people live year-round in the high country; those who do must use its resources intensively for agriculture and husbandry. This puts pressure on wild prey animals. As their numbers decline, the snow leopards turn to livestock, which can be a heavy blow -- $50 to $300 annually, in some places -- for pastoralists who are only making between $250 and $400 per year. (*Jackson et al.*)

The top-down approach to conservation -- "fences and guns," as some call it -- doesn't work in the snow leopard's unique geopolitical setting.

Instead, this big cat's best chances for protection come from local people, even though these are the ones who are hardest hit by snow leopard predation.

To prevent retaliation and persecution of snow leopards, some countries have programs in place to compensate livestock owners, as well as to promote more effective ways to protect livestock.

And some local communities have gained economic benefit from having such big cats as neighbors, thanks to all the tourists who come to see wild snow leopards.

Ecotourism income can balance out or, sometimes, even surpass losses from snow leopard predation on livestock.

It isn't easy to implement such community-level conservation measures, but such efforts are showing some promise.

Red-listed?

Snow leopards are listed as Vulnerable. They were downlisted from Endangered in 2015 when it was established that there were more than 2,500 adults left in the wild.

But with fewer than 10,000 mature individuals possibly out there right now, snow leopards are still at risk of extinction.

There is also concern that, for a variety of reasons, wild snow leopard numbers will drop significantly over the next two decades. (See the Cat Specialist Group at http://www.catsg.org/index.php?id=100 and the IUCN at

https://www.iucnredlist.org/species/22732/50664030
for details.)

Fossil relatives

Given the ruggedness of their environment, it's not surprising to hear that snow leopards haven 't left much of a record in the rocky archives.

Recent fossil discoveries in Tibet suggest that the tiger/snow leopard line may go back at least four million years to an ancient big cat called *Panthera blytheae*.

Whether it was closely related to snow leopards or more of a distant connection depends on which source you check. (*Tseng et al.; Wang et al.*)

Either way, this big cat lived in early Pliocene to times, or possibly even in the late Miocene, and its remains have been found along with those of ancestors of the wild sheep that today's snow leopards hunt.

More recent fossils, from the Pleistocene ice ages, have

been found in Altai mountain caves and connected to snow leopards. Others are known from northern Pakistan. (*Turner and Antón*)

However, Werdelin *et al.* note that these Pleistocene finds are all teeth. Since taxonomists rely on physical anatomy (i.e., the bony skeleton), it's very difficult to prove beyond a shadow of a doubt that they belong to Uncia.

Believe it or not, there is a cat that's even less well understand than the snow leopard. It lives closer to sea level, but it's extremely shy and wary . . .

Hyperlinks

- *Video*: Snow leopard chuffing:
  https://www.youtube.com/watch?v=0cCDqbiGvoQ

- *Video*: Wild snow leopard, scent marking:
  https://youtu.be/NPvpR_iMB2M

- *Video*: Snow leopard ecotourism:
  https://youtu.be/AuXVJi_2t5U

Charlie Marshall, CC BY 2.0, https://www.flickr.com/photos/100915417@N07/40996036275

Clouded leopards

Don't feel bad if you've never heard of clouded leopards before. These rare predators, hidden deep inside Asia's rainforests, puzzle professionals, too.

 Note the splotches on that coat -- those are the "clouds" this adorable cat is named for. (Image: Charlie Marshall, CC BY 2.0, https://www.flickr.com/photos/100915417@N07/41660423014)

But the "leopard" part? It's difficult to avoid that in a spotted big cat.

Nevertheless, for a long time experts didn't believe clouded leopards belonged in Panthera alongside "real" leopards.

After all, clouded leopards don't roar; they purr. And they only top the scale at around 50 pounds -- some are even smaller than that!

Yet in many respects clouded leopards *do* act like a big cat. (*Cat Specialist Group*)

Down through the years, some zoologists chose to group clouded leopards together with nonpantherine cats (*Heptner and Sludskii*), while others considered this species to be a transitional form between Panthera and the rest of family Felidae -- sort of a "small big cat." (*Macdonald et al.; Sunquist and Sunquist*)

Then genetic testing in the early 2000s eventually settled the matter: clouded leopards, though small, are indeed pantherines.

But there is still much more -- including basic information like how many clouded leopards are left and how they behave in the wild -- that conservationists need to know.

Scientific name: *Neofelis nebulosa.*

Here's another complexity accompanying clouded leopards.

Legislation that protects these gorgeous pantherines (image by Eric Kilby, CC BY-SA 2.0, 
https://www.flickr.com/photos/ekilby/8429101030) and also covers other endangered animals and plants (CITES, or the Convention on International Trade in Endangered Species of Wild Fauna and Flora) identifies clouded leopards as *N. nebulosa*.

But for over a decade, many professional cat herders have been using two scientific names:

1. Mainland clouded leopard (*N. nebulosa*): All of them

except those on the Sunda islands.

2. Sunda clouded leopard (*N. diardi*): The island clouded leopards, found today on Sumatra and Borneo (and perhaps the Batu Islands, though this hasn't been documented yet). Up until this point, these had been called a subspecies, *N. nebulosa diardi*.

These developed out of the same genetic studies that placed clouded leopards among the big cats (starting in 2006).

Those studies not only established the clouded leopard's place in the cat family tree but also identified these two separate species. Other researchers have backed this up by describing anatomical differences between *N. nebulosa* and *N. diardi*.

It could have happened, according to the biological species concept, which predicts that new species appear after some of the older species get isolated from the rest and continue to evolve on their own.

Not much water covers the Sunda Shelf today, and it was sometimes dry land during the ice ages.

During those times, enough clouded leopards to found a breeding population could have wandered onto what are now the islands of Sumatra and Borneo, getting cut off by rising sea levels as the great continental ice fields closer to Earth's poles melted away.

"Ize a mainland kitteh. Sunda too far to walk" – Clouded leopard. (Image: Charles Barilleaux, CC BY 2.0, https://www.flickr.com/photos/bontempscharly/7750524126)

They could no longer exchange genes with the mainland clouded leopards and so started off on their own evolutionary path.

Some of today's cat experts find enough differences now to call the Sunda clouded leopards a new species. However, I'm still going to continue to talk about *the* clouded leopard, *N. nebulosa*, since CITES terminology still calls it a single species.

I know that there are more ways to define a species than just reproductive isolation. No one way is "right" -- it all depends on the purposes behind the definition (*de Queiroz*).

Physical differences do matter to taxonomists (the specialists who decide what scientific names are most accurate), but to this layperson differences described between mainland and Sunda clouded leopards seem very subtle.

And from what little has been reported widely of mainland and Sunda clouded leopard ecology, the two seem to live in almost identical ways.

Nor have I come across anything discussing interbreeding between mainland and Sunda clouded leopards.

So little is known about wild clouded leopards that I suspect the last word on Neofelis species/subspecies has yet to be written.

In the meantime, though it's never helpful for a layperson to second-guess specialists, it's not wrong to continue following the approach used in legislation that protects clouded leopards.

Just be sure also to check out sources that view clouded leopards as two separate species. Online resources range from the general -- Wikipedia's mainland and Sunda clouded leopard pages, for example -- to science-based authorities like the Cat Specialist Group, which discusses mainland http://www.catsg.org/index.php?id=116 and

Sunda http://www.catsg.org/index.php?id=225 clouded leopards separately.

Data

These are from the Cat Specialist Group unless otherwise noted. (Image by Tambako the Jaguar, CC BY-ND 2.0,

https://www.flickr.com/photos/tambako/34020184264)

- **Weight:** Mainland: 35 to 51 pounds. Sunda: 24 to 55 pounds.

- **Height at the shoulder:** Mainland: 20 to 22 inches. (*Wikipedia; not given on Sunda clouded leopard*)

- **Body length:** For both: 27 to 43 inches.

- Tail length: For both: 24 to 36 inches. Clouded leopards are quite at home in trees and use this extra-long tail for balance. Other adaptations to the arboreal lifestyle include very broad paws and short, stout legs.

- Coat: Words just can't convey the beauty of that coat on any clouded leopard, with its clouds, stripes, and spots on a background that can range from yellowish-brown to dark gray. As with most wild cats, the underparts are lighter colored and the back of each ear shows a light area set in very dark fur. Per Allen et al., individual clouded leopards can be identified by their coat patterns. Per the Cat Specialist Group, Sunda clouded leopards have smaller "clouds" and a grayer background than their mainland relatives. Sunquist and Sunquist note that all-black (melanistic) clouded leopards are extremely rare but have been reported from Borneo.

- Vocals: Clouded leopards make most of the same sounds that small cats do, including purring. But they also respond to chuffing. Clouded leopards reportedly have a drawn-out moaning call that can be heard at some distance. (*Sunquist and Sunquist*)

- Average litter size: Both: 1 to 2 cubs. Ewer notes

that this ranges from 1 to 4 cubs; typically, 2 cubs are born.

- Average life span: Mainland: 15 to 17 years. Sunda: 11 years on average, up to 17 years. (This may be data from captives, since very little is known about wild clouded leopards.)

Features unique to clouded leopards

Eric Kilby, CC BY-SA 2.0, https://www.flickr.com/photos/ekilby/39295957402

- The longest fangs of any cat, in proportion to body size. Yes, tigers have the longest fangs overall, but they're also very large cats. Canines pushing 2 inches long (*Macdonald et al.*) are very unusual to see on a 50-pound cat! However, it's important to note that these aren't saberteeth. For one thing, they're conical in shape; sabercat upper canines were flat as well as long. For another, the clouded leopard also has dramatic lower fangs, where sabertoothed cats often had unusually small lower canines.

- The only big cat able to rotate its ankles 180 degrees and come headfirst out of a tree. A couple of the smaller cats -- margays and marbled cats -- can do this, too. Sunquist and Sunquist describe clouded leopards hanging from branches by their hind feet!

- According to many molecular studies, the oldest line of descent in modern cats, going back at least five million years and probably more than that. (*Christiansen, 2008a; Kitchener et al., 2017; Werdelin et al.*) Hmm, that oddly primitive appearance in clouded leopards makes a little more sense now.

- It's true that clouded leopards are the only big cat

with a clouded coat, but a much smaller Southeast Asian feline, the marbled cat, has one just like it. Werdelin *et al.* note that the marbled cat's lineage is the oldest in its group (which is one of seven other "branches" in the cat family besides Panthera). They speculate that this blotchy coat pattern, whether you call it "clouds" or "marbling," might be the one originally sported by all early members of family Felidae!

Where found in the wild

Clouded leopards avoid people and live in the densest part of a forest -- usually, but not always tropical rainforest (image by BhagyaMani via Wikimedia, CC BY -SA 4.0,

https://commons.wikimedia.org/wiki/File:Clouded-leopard_distribution.jpg#mw-jump-to-license).

Camera trapping has provided some data on them to

supplement the occasional sighting. But only a little.

Cameras work the best when placed on well-traveled trails. But clouded leopards often travel through the trees, where there are no trails to guide camera trap setups. (*Haidir et al.*)

That said, clouded leopards have been observed from the Himalayan foothills in Nepal (up to 8,000 feet or more) through mainland Southeast Asia into China and southward into peninsular Malaysia, Sumatra, and Borneo.

Those on the island of Java disappeared during Neolithic times. Some sources say that clouded leopards are extinct in Singapore and Taiwan, but there are some recent reports that mention Taiwan's wild clouded leopards, so I'm not sure what the status is there.

Closest cat family relatives

DNA markers show that clouded leopards are separate

from the other pantherines. They have no closer connection to leopards than they do to lions, tigers, jaguars, or snow leopards.

Panthera is the oldest branch on the modern cat family tree, and clouded leopards are the oldest line on this branch. Apparently their ancestors evolved first; a little bit later (but still VERY long ago), those of the rest of today's big cats appeared and went their slightly different ways.

Famous clouded leopards

Zookeepers are very proud of clouded leopards Chai Li and Nah Fun, who live at Tacoma's Point Defiance Zoo and Aquarium and have produced four litters thus far (check out hyperlinks below to see a video of some of their cubs).

Chai Li and Nah Fun have even been covered in Time magazine!

How clouded leopards hunt and eat

This is a very short section. So little is known about clouded leopards, no one is even speculating about why they have evolved such long teeth!

Check out the references given for this chapter at the end of the book for some papers that discuss clouded leopard habitat, hunting habits, and prey. As of the time of writing, there are too few studies to base any broad generalizations on here.

These beautiful pantherines aren't solely restricted to the depth of a primeval tropical rainforest, but they do avoid people and seem to prefer the densest parts of any forested region. This makes it very difficult to study them in the wild.

How they reproduce

This information is probably from observing captive clouded leopards.

After a three-month gestation, cubs are usually born in the spring (March through June). They weight only 5 to 10 ounces at birth and have spotted coats; the glorious "clouds" take about six months to develop.

Cubs open their eyes during the first two weeks of life, and in another week can walk around. Suckling will continue until around age three months, but the cubs start taking meat when they are seven to ten months old.

Sunquist and Sunquist note that cubs can kill a chicken when 80 days old, which seems a little precocious compared to other big cats. Per the Cat Specialist Group, it takes mainland clouded leopards a little over two years to reach sexual maturity.

Interactions with people

Clouded leopards are the state animal of Meghalaya, in India.

Per the Cat Specialist Group, Sunda clouded leopards on Borneo sometimes go after domestic livestock, but this is rare and retaliation killing is uncommon. Otherwise, I could find little information about human-cat conflict or any other interactions involving clouded leopards, apart from illegal hunting and trade in pelts and body parts, which continues despite international and local conservation laws.

Red-listed?

The International Union for the Conservation of Nature (IUCN) lists both mainland https://www.iucnredlist.org/species/14519/97215090 and Sunda clouded leopards https://www.iucnredlist.org/species/136603/97212874 as vulnerable, for detailed reasons given at those links.

They also note that conservationists in Nepal consider the clouded leopard there to be endangered.

But the IUCN, like the Cat Specialist Group and other authorities, emphasizes that much more needs to be learned about wild clouded leopards to understand exactly what their risk for extinction may be and what steps to protect them would work the best.

Fossil relatives

The humid tropical forests that clouded leopards call home are beautiful but they don't preserve remains very well.

Some fossil teeth going back almost 900,000 years have been identified (*Johnson et al.; Werdelin et al.*), but thus far nothing older has been found

Such finds do show that clouded leopards once roamed the island of Java, though they have been extinct there since the Neolithic. (*Cat Specialist Group*)

Hyperlinks

- *Video*: Clouded leopards respond to chuffing: https://youtu.be/lubJ3rd84ws

- *Web page*: Time magazine 2015 article on clouded leopard cubs: https://time.com/3890508/clouded-leopard-cubs-quadruplets/

- *Video*: Clouded leopard cubs in the Tacoma zoo: https://youtu.be/v2pz2iphwAg

Afterword

Sometimes it's best to just stop talking, when you're on a deep subject, and let people absorb what they have heard.

Anything having to do with family Felidae is deep, not to mention complicated and incompletely understood.

Much cutting-edge research about cats is ongoing in a variety of fields, including (but definitely not limited to) paleontology, molecular biology, zoology, and wildlife management.

Here, hopefully, I've accomplished my goal of getting you even more interested in big cats with this introduction.

I'm now going to get to work on another book, this time about the 30-some other species in the modern cat family. After that will come the sabercats. (Follow this progress, if you want, at my blog https://flighttowonder.com/.)

In the meantime, all around us every day, the cat family story goes on and on.

The following reference section, in addition to the main text, will help you on your way if you decide to get better acquainted with lions, tigers, leopards, jaguars, snow leopards, and/or clouded leopards.

You also now have some sweet images to enjoy, over and over again, thanks to all the wonderful photographers who were willing to share their work with the world.

References

Lions:

Bauer, H.; Packer, C.; Funston, P.F.; Henschel, P.; and Nowell, K. 2016. *Panthera leo* (errata version published in 2017). *The IUCN Red List of Threatened Species 2016*: e.T15951A115130419. https://www.iucnredlist.org/species/15951/115130419

Bocherens, H. 2015. Isotopic tracking of large carnivore palaeoecology in the mammoth steppe. *Quaternary Science Reviews*, 117: 42-71.

Breitenmoser, U.; Mallon, D.P.; Ahmad Khan, J.; and Driscoll, C. 2008. *Panthera leo ssp. persica. The IUCN Red List of Threatened Species 2008*: e.T15952A5327221. https://www.iucnredlist.org/species/15952/5327221

Cat Specialist Group. 2019. African lion. http://www.catsg.org/index.php?id=108 Last accessed March 5, 2019.

___. 2019. Asiatic lion. http://www.catsg.org/index.php?id=113 Last accessed March 5, 2019.

Christiansen, P. 2008. Phylogeny of the great cats (Felidae: Pantherinae), and the influence of fossil taxa and missing characters. *Cladistics*, 24(6): 977-992.

Cincinnati Zoo & Botanical Garden. 2019. White lion.

http://cincinnatizoo.org/animals/white-lion-2/ Last accessed October 24, 2019.

Craft, M. E. 2010. Ecology of infectious diseases in Serengeti lions, in Biology and Conservation of Wild Felids, ed. Macdonald, D. W., and Loveridge, A. J., 263-281. Oxford: Oxford University Press.

Ewer, R. F. 1973. The carnivores. The World Naturalist, ed. Carrington, R. London: Weidenfeld and Nicolson.

Figueiró, H. V.; Li, G.; Trindade, F. J.; Assis, J.; and others. 2017. Genome-wide signatures of complex introgression and adaptive evolution in the big cats. Science Advances, 3(7): e1700299.

Johnson, W. E.; Eizirik, E.; Pecon-Slattery, J.; Murphy, W. J.; and others. 2006. The Late Miocene radiation of modern Felidae: A genetic assessment. Science, 311: 73-77.

King, L. M. 2012. Phylogeny of Panthera, Including P. atrox, Based on Cranialmandibular Characters. Electronic Theses and Dissertations. Paper 1444. http://dc.etsu.edu/etd/1444

Kitchener, A. C.; Van Valkenburgh, B.; and Yamaguchi, N. 2010. Felid form and function, in Biology and Conservation of Wild Felids, ed. Macdonald, D. W., and Loveridge, A. J., 83-106. Oxford: Oxford University Press.

Kitchener, A. C.; Breitenmoser-Würsten, C.; Eizirik, E.; Gentry, A.; and others. 2017. A revised taxonomy of the Felidae: The final report of the Cat Classification Task Force of the IUCN Cat Specialist Group. https://repository.si.edu/bitstream/handle/10088/32616/A_revised_Felidae_Taxonomy_CatNews.pdf

Li, G.; Davis, B. W.; Eizirik, E.; and Murphy, W. J. 2016. Phylogenomic evidence for ancient hybridization in the genomes of living cats (Felidae). Genome Research, 26(1): 1-11.

Loveridge, A.; Wang, S. W.; Frank, L.; and Seidensticker, J. 2010. People and wild felids: conservation of cats and management of conflicts, in Biology and Conservation of Wild Felids, eds. Macdonald, D. W., and Loveridge, A. J., 161-195. Oxford: Oxford University Press.

Loveridge, A. J.; Hemson, G.; Davidson, Z.; and Macdonald, D. W. 2010a. African lions on the edge: reserve boundaries as 'attractive sinks', in Biology and Conservation of Wild Felids, eds. Macdonald, D. W., and Loveridge, A. J., 283-304. Oxford: Oxford University Press.

Macdonald, D. W.; Loveridge, A. J.; and Nowell, K. 2010a. Dramatis personae: An introduction to the wild felids, in Biology and Conservation of Wild Felids, eds. Macdonald, D. W., and Loveridge, A. J., 3-58. Oxford: Oxford University Press.

Macdonald, D. W;, Mosser, A.; and Gittleman, J. L. 2010b. Felid society, in Biology and Conservation of Wild Felids, eds. Macdonald, D. W., and Loveridge, A. J., 125-160. Oxford: Oxford University Press.

Macdonald, D. W.; Loveridge, A. J.; and Rabinowitz, A. 2010c. Felid futures: crossing disciplines, borders, and generations, in Biology and Conservation of Wild Felids, eds. Macdonald, D. W., and Loveridge, A. J., 599. Oxford: Oxford University Press.

Motsinger, C. 2018. Two of the rarest animals in the planet are in Cincinnati. But maybe not for long. https://www.cincinnati.com/story/news/2018/09/26/cincinnati-zoo-home-maybe-oldest-white-lions-earth/1283501002/ Last accessed October 24, 2019.

National Sleep Foundation. 2019. These kings of the jungle get quite a bit of shut-eye! https://www.sleep.org/articles/sleep-habits-of-lions/ Last accessed October 24, 2019.

Nyakatura, K., and Bininda-Emonds, O. R. P. 2012. Updating the evolutionary history of Carnivora (Mammalia): a new species-level supertree complete with divergence time estimates. BMC Biology. 10:12.

O'Brien, S. J., and Johnson, W. E. 2007. The evolution of cats. Scientific American, 297 (1): 68-75..

Stuart, A. J. 2015. Late Quaternary megafaunal extinctions on the continents: a short review. Geological Journal, 50(3): 338-363.

Sunquist, M. and Sunquist, F. 2002. *Wild Cats of the World. Chicago and London: University of Chicago Press. Retrieved from https://play.google.com/store/books/details?id=IF8nDwAAQBAJ*

Turner, A., and Antón, M. 1997. *The Big Cats and Their Fossil Relatives: An Illustrated Guide to Their Evolution and Natural History. New York: Columbia University Press.*

Werdelin, L.; Yamaguchi, N.; Johnson, W. E.; and O'Brien, S. J.. 2010. *Phylogeny and evolution of cats (Felidae), in Biology and Conservation of Wild Felids, eds. Macdonald, D. W., and Loveridge, A. J., 59-82. Oxford: Oxford University Press.*

Werdelin, L., and Dehghani, R. 2011. *Carnivora, in Paleontology and Geology of Laetoli: Human Evolution in Context, Volume 2: Fossil Hominins and the Associated Fauna, Harrison, T., ed., 189-232. Springer, Dordrecht.*

Wikipedia. 2019. *Christian the lion. https://en.wikipedia.org/wiki/Christian_the_lion   Last accessed October 24, 2019.*

___. 2019. *Elsa the lioness. https://en.wikipedia.org/wiki/Elsa_the_lioness Last accessed October 24, 2019.*

___. 2019. *Lion. https://en.wikipedia.org/wiki/Lion Last accessed October 25, 2019.*

___. 2019. *White lion. https://en.wikipedia.org/wiki/White_lion Last accessed October 24, 2019.*

Allen, W. L.; Cuthill, I. C.; Scott-Samuel, N. E.; and Baddeley, R. 2011. Why the leopard got its spots: relating pattern development to ecology in felids. Proceedings of the Royal Society B, 278: 1373-1380.

Amur Tiger Center. 2018. Saving Russian Heritage Together (Russian and English) http://amur-tiger.ru/data/report-2018.pdf

Animal Fair. 2015. Las Vegas Icons Siegfried And Roy – Where Are The Tigers Now? https://animalfair.com/2015/10/19/siegfried-roy-tigers-now/ Last accessed October 29, 2019.

Cat Specialist Group. 2019. Tiger. http://www.catsg.org/index.php?id=124 Last accessed May 17, 2019.

Cho, Y. S.; Hu, L.; Hou, H.; Lee, H.; and others. 2013. The tiger genome and comparative analysis with lions and snow leopard genomes. Nature Communications, 4: 24-33.

Chowdhury, A. N.; Brahma, A.; Mondal, R.; and Biswas, M. K. 2016. Stigma of tiger attack: Study of tiger-widows from Sundarban Delta, India. Journal of Indian Psychiatry, 58(1): 12-19.

Chundawat, R. S.; Khan, J. A.; and Mallon, D. P. 2011. Panthera tigris ssp. tigris. The IUCN Red List of Threatened Species 2011:e.T136899A4348945.

Christiansen, P. 2008. Phylogeny of the great cats (Felidae: Pantherinae), and the influence of fossil taxa and missing characters. Cladistics, 24(6): 977-992.

Culver, M.; Driscoll, C.; Eizirik, E.; and Spong, G. 2010. Genetic applications in wild felids, in Biology and Conservation of Wild Felids, ed. Macdonald, D. W., and Loveridge, A. J., 107-124. Oxford: Oxford University Press.

Das, C. S. 2018. Pattern and characterisation of human casualties in Sundarban by tiger attacks, India. Sustainable Forestry, 1(2):1-10.

Davis, B. W.; Li, G.; and Murphy. W. J. 2010. Supermatrix and species tree methods resolve phylogenetic relationships within the big cats, Panthera (Carnivora: Felidae). Molecular Phylogenetics and Evolution, 56(1): 64-76.

Dhungana, R.; Savini, T.; Karki, J. B.; Dhakal, M.; and others. 2018. Living with tigers Panthera tigris: patterns, correlates, and contexts of human−tiger conflict in Chitwan National Park, Nepal. Oryx, 52(1): 55-65.

Ewer, R. F. 1973. The carnivores. The World Naturalist, ed. Carrington, R. London: Weidenfeld and Nicolson.

Godfrey, D.; Lythgoe, J. N.; and Rumball, D. A. 1987. Zebra stripes and tiger stripes: the spatial frequency distribution of the pattern compared to that of the background is significant in display and crypsis. Biological Journal of the Linnaean Society, 32(4): 427-433.

Goodrich, J.; Lynam, A.; Miguelle, D.; Wibisono, H.; and others. 2015. Panthera tigris. The IUCN Red List of Threatened Species 2015:3.T15955A50659951.

Goswami, U. 2019. View: Doubling tiger population laudable but India needs to do more. https://economictimes.indiatimes.com/news/science/view-doubling-tiger-population-laudable-but-india-needs-to-do-more/articleshow/70435503.cms?from=mdr Last accessed October 29, 2019.

Haslam, M., and Petraglia, M. 2010. Comment on "Environmental impact of the 73 ka Toba super-eruption in South Asia" by MAJ Williams, SH Ambrose, S. van der Kaars, C. Ruehlemann, U. Chattopadhyaya, J. Pal and PR Chauhan [Palaeogeography, Palaeoclimatology, Palaeoecology 284 (2009) 295–314]. Palaeogeography, Palaeoclimatology, Palaeoecology, 296(1-2): 199-203.

Heptner, V. G., and Sludskii, A. A. 1972. Mammals of the Soviet Union, volume II, part 2: Carnivora (hyaenas and cats). Moscow: Vysshaya Shkola Publishers. English translation by Rao, P.M., 1992. General editor: Kothekar, V. S. New Delhi: Amerind Publishing. https://archive.org/details/mammalsofsov221992gept

Herbst, M. 2009. Behavioural ecology and population genetics of the African wild cat, Felis silvestris Forster 1870, in the southern Kalahari. PhD thesis, University of Pretoria.

Heske, E. J. Fall 2013 semester. Mammalogy 462, online class notes. Carnivora Suborder Feliformia *http://www.life.illinois.edu/ib/462/Lab%2019%20Carnivora1.pdf Last accessed October 30, 2019.*

Johnson, W. E.; Eizirik, E.; Pecon-Slattery, J.; Murphy, W. J.; and others. 2006. The Late Miocene radiation of modern Felidae: A enetic assessment. Science, 311: 73-77.

Kitchener, A. C., Van Valkenburgh, B., and Yamaguchi, N. 2010. Felid form and function. In Biology and Conservation of Wild Felids, ed. D. W. Macdonald and A. J. Loveridge, 83106. Oxford: Oxford University Press, Oxford.

Kitchener, A. C., and Yamaguchi, N. 2010. What is a tiger? Biogeography, morphology, and taxonomy, in Tigers of the World (pp. 53-84). William Andrew Publishing.

Kitchener, A. C.; Breitenmoser-Würsten, C.; Eizirik, E.; Gentry, A.; and others. 2017. A revised taxonomy of the Felidae: The final report of the Cat Classification Task Force of the IUCN Cat Specialist Group. https://repository.si.edu/bitstream/handle/10088/32616/A_revised_Felidae_Taxonomy_CatNews.pdf

Kupferschmidt, K. 2015. Controversial study claims there are only two types of tigers. https://www.sciencemag.org/news/2015/06/controversial-study-claims-there-are-only-two-types-tiger Last accessed November 6, 2019.

Linkie, M.; Wibisono, H. T.; Martyr, D. J.; and Sunarto, S. 2008. Panthera tigris ssp. sumatrae. The IUCN Red List of Threatened Species 2008:e.T15966A5334836. https://www.iucnredlist.org/species/15966/5334836

Louys, J. 2012. Mammal community structure of Sundanese fossil assemblages from the Late Pleistocene, and a discussion on the ecological effects of the Toba eruption. Quaternary International, 258: 80-87.

Loveridge, A.; Wang, S. W.; Frank, L.; and Seidensticker, J. 2010. People and wild felids: conservation of cats and management of conflicts, in Biology and Conservation of Wild Felids, eds. Macdonald, D. W., and Loveridge, A. J., 161-195. Oxford: Oxford University Press.

Luo, S. J.; Kim, J. H.; Johnson, W. E.; Van Der Walt, J.; and others. 2004. Phylogeography and genetic ancestry of tigers (Panthera tigris). PLoS Biology, 2(12): e442.

Luo, S-J., and Xu, X. 2014. Save the White Tigers. Scientific American, https://www.scientificamerican.com/article/save-the-white-tigers/ Last accessed November 6, 2019.

Macdonald, D. W.; Loveridge, A. J.; and Nowell, K. 2010. Dramatis personae: An introduction to the wild felids, in Biology and Conservation of Wild Felids, eds. Macdonald, D. W., and Loveridge, A. J., 3-58. Oxford: Oxford University Press.

Macdonald, D. W;, Mosser, A.; and Gittleman, J. L. 2010a. Felid society, in Biology and Conservation of Wild Felids, eds. Macdonald, D. W., and Loveridge, A. J., 125-160. Oxford: Oxford University Press.

Macdonald, D. W.; Loveridge, A. J.; and Rabinowitz, A. 2010b. Felid futures: crossing disciplines, borders, and generations, in Biology and Conservation of Wild Felids, eds. Macdonald, D. W., and Loveridge, A. J., 599. Oxford: Oxford University Press.

Mazák, J. H. 2010. Craniometric variation in the tiger (Panthera tigris): Implications for patterns of diversity, taxonomy and conservation. Mammalian Biology-Zeitschrift für Säugetierkunde, 75(1): 45-68.

Mazak, J. H. 2010a. What is Panthera palaeosinensis?. Mammal Review, 40(1): 90-102.

Mazák, J. H.; Christiansen, P.; and Kitchener, A. C. 2012 Correction: Oldest Known Pantherine Skull and Evolution of the Tiger. PLOS ONE 7(1): 10.1371/annotation/a60b7ac3-7f06-465b-a8df-2f359d59a021.

Miquelle, D. G.; Goodrich, J. M.; Smirnov, E. N.; Stephens, P. A.; and others. 2010. The Amur tiger: a case study of living on the edge, in Biology and Conservation of Wild Felids, eds. Macdonald, D. W., and Loveridge, A. J., 325-339. Oxford: Oxford University Press.

Nyakatura, K., and Bininda-Emonds, O. R. P. 2012. Updating the evolutionary history of Carnivora (Mammalia): a new species-level supertree complete with divergence time estimates. BMC Biology, 10:12.

O'Brien, S. J., and Johnson, W. E. 2005. Big cat genomics. Annual Review of Genomics and Human Genetics. 6:407-429.

O'Brien, S. J., and Johnson, W. E. 2007. The evolution of cats. Scientific American. 297 (1):68-75.

Oñoz-Wright, A. 2015. Siegfried & Roy welcome four tiger cubs. https://blog.vegas.com/las-vegas-attractions/siegfried-roy-welcome-four-tiger-cubs-60811/ Last accessed October 29, 2019.

Sanderson, E.; Forrest, J.; Loucks, C.; Ginsberg, J.; and others. 2010. "Setting priorities for conservation and recovery of wild tigers: 2005-2015. The technical assessment." in Tigers of theworld: the science, politics, and conservation of Panthera tigris, edited by Tilson, Ronald Lewis and Nyhus, Philip J., Second ed. 143–161. New York: Elsevier/Academic Press. Downloaded from https://repository.si.edu/handle/10088/11080

Schneider, A.; Henegar, C.; Day, K.; Absher, D.; and others. 2015. Recurrent evolution of melanism in South American felids. PLoS Genetics. 11(2): e1004892.

Seidensticker, J.; Dinerstein, E.; Goyal, S. P.; Gurung, B.; and others. 2010. Tiger range collapse and recovery at the base of the Himalayas, in Biology and Conservation of Wild Felids, eds. Macdonald, D. W., and Loveridge, A. J., 305-324. Oxford: Oxford University Press.

St. Petersburg Declaration (English). 2010. http://cmsdata.iucn.org/downloads/st_petersburg_declaration_english.pdf

Sunquist, M. and Sunquist, F. 2002. Wild Cats of the World. Chicago and London: University of Chicago Press. Retrieved from https://play.google.com/store/books/details?id=IF8nDwAAQBAJ

Thakur, J. February 3, 2017. In Sunderbans, no one cares about villagers who go missing in animal attacks. http://www.hindustantimes.com/india-news/in-sunderbans-no-one-cares-about-villagers-who-go-missing-in-animal-attacks/story-qBfi3zcR9OnU0EZXNgGNyJ.html Last accessed September 13, 2017.

Tseng, Z. J.; Wang, X.; Slater, G. J.; Takeuchi, G. T.; and others. 2014. Himalayan fossils of the oldest known pantherine establish ancient origin of big cats. Proceedings of the Royal Society B: Biological Sciences, 281(1774): 20132686.

Turner, A., and Antón, M. 1997. The Big Cats and Their Fossil Relatives: An Illustrated Guide to Their Evolution and Natural History. New York: Columbia University Press.

Werdelin, L., and Olsson, L. 1997. How the leopard got its spots: a phylogenetic view off the evolution of felid coat patterns. Biological Journal of the Linnaean Society. 62: 383-400

Werdelin, L.; Yamaguchi, N.; Johnson, W. E.; and O'Brien, S. J. 2010. Phylogeny and evolution of cats (Felidae), in Biology and Conservation of Wild Felids, eds. Macdonald, D. W., and Loveridge, A. J., 59-82. Oxford: Oxford University Press.

Wikipedia. 2019. Captive white tigers. https://en.wikipedia.org/wiki/Captive_white_tigers Last accessed November 6, 2019.

___. 2019. *Siegfried & Roy.*
https://en.wikipedia.org/wiki/Siegfried_%26_Roy *Last accessed October 24, 2019.*

___. 2019. *Tiger. https://en.wikipedia.org/wiki/Tiger Last accessed October 26, 2019.*

___. 2019. *Tiger conservation.*
https://en.wikipedia.org/wiki/Tiger_conservation Last accessed October 29, 2019.

Williams, M. A.; Ambrose, S. H.; van der Kaars, S.; Ruehlemann, C.; and others. 2009. Environmental impact of the 73 ka Toba super-eruption in South Asia. Palaeogeography, Palaeoclimatology, Palaeoecology, 284(3-4): 295-314.

World Wildlife Fund. 2018. Nepal set to become the first country to double its tigers. https://www.worldwildlife.org/press-releases/nepal-set-to-become-first-country-to-double-wild-tiger-population Last accessed October 29, 2019.

Xu, X.; Dong, G. X.; Hu, X. S.; Miao, L.; and others. 2013. The genetic basis of white tigers. CurrentBbiology, 23(11): 1031-1035.

Allen, W. L.; Cuthill, I. C.; Scott-Samuel, N. E.; and Baddeley, R. 2011. Why the leopard got its spots: relating pattern development to ecology in felids. Proceedings of the Royal Society B, 278: 1373-1380.

Athreya, V.; Odden, M.; Linnell, J. D.; and Karanth, K. U. 2011. Translocation as a tool for mitigating conflict with leopards in human-dominated landscapes of India. Conservation Biology, 25(1): 133-141.

Barnosky, A. D.; Koch, P. L.; Feranec, R. S.; Wing, S. L.; and Shabel, A. B. 2004. Assessing the causes of late Pleistocene extinctions on the continents. Science, 306(5693): 70-75.

Cat Specialist Group. 2019. Leopard. http://www.catsg.org/index.php?id=110 Last accessed August 14, 2019.

Davis, B. W.; Li, G.; and Murphy. W. J. 2010. Supermatrix and species tree methods resolve phylogenetic relationships within the big cats, Panthera (Carnivora: Felidae). Molecular Phylogenetics and Evolution, 56(1): 64-76.

Eizirik, E.; Yuhki, N.; Johnson, W. E.; Menotti-Raymond, M.; and others. 2003. Molecular genetics and evolution of melanism in the cat family. Current Biology, 13(5): 448-453.

Ewer, R. F. 1973. The carnivores. The World Naturalist, ed. Carrington, R.

London: Weidenfeld and Nicolson.

Figueiró, H. V.; Li, G.; Trindade, F. J.; Assis, J.; and others. 2017. Genome-wide signatures of complex introgression and adaptive evolution in the big cats. *Science Advances*, 3(7): e1700299.

Ghezzo, E., and Rook, L. 2015. The remarkable *Panthera pardus* (Felidae, Mammalia) record from Equi (Massa, Italy): taphonomy, morphology, and paleoecology. *Quaternary Science Reviews*, 110: 131-151.

Hedges, L.; Lam, W. Y.; Campos-Arceiz, A.; Rayan, D. M.; and others. 2015. Melanistic leopards reveal their spots: Infrared camera traps provide a population density estimate of leopards in Malaysia. Abstract only *The Journal of Wildlife Management*, 79(5): 846-853.

Heptner, V. G., and Sludskii, A. A. 1972. *Mammals of the Soviet Union, volume II, part 2: Carnivora (hyaenas and cats)*. Moscow: Vysshaya Shkola Publishers. English translation by Rao, P.M., 1992. General editor: Kothekar, V. S. New Delhi: Amerind Publishing. https://archive.org/details/mammalsofsov221992gept

Jacobson, A. P.; Gerngross, P.; Lemeris Jr, J. R.; Schoonover, R. F.; and others. 2016. Leopard (*Panthera pardus*) status, distribution, and the research efforts across its range. *PeerJ 4 : e1974*.

Johnson, W. E.; Eizirik, E.; Pecon-Slattery, J.; Murphy, W. J.; and others.

2006. The Late Miocene radiation of modern Felidae: A genetic assessment. Science, 311: 73-77.

Kawanishi, K.; Sunquist, M. E.; Eizirik, E.; Lynam, A. J.; and others. 2010. Near fixation of melanism in leopards of the Malay Peninsula. Journal of Zoology, 282(3): 201-206.

Kitchener, A. C.; Van Valkenburgh, B.; and Yamaguchi, N. 2010. Felid form and function, in Biology and Conservation of Wild Felids, ed. Macdonald, D. W., and Loveridge, A. J., 83-106. Oxford: Oxford University Press.

Kitchener, A. C.; Breitenmoser-Würsten, C.; Eizirik, E.; Gentry, A.; and others. 2017. A revised taxonomy of the Felidae: The final report of the Cat Classification Task Force of the IUCN Cat Specialist Group. https://repository.si.edu/bitstream/handle/10088/32616/A_revised_Felida e_Taxonomy_CatNews.pdf

Macdonald, D. W.; Loveridge, A. J.; and Nowell, K. 2010. Dramatis personae: An introduction to the wild felids, in Biology and Conservation of Wild Felids, eds. Macdonald, D. W., and Loveridge, A. J., 3-58. Oxford: Oxford University Press.

Nyakatura, K., and Bininda-Emonds, O. R. P. 2012. Updating the evolutionary history of Carnivora (Mammalia): a new species-level supertree complete with divergence time estimates. BMC Biology, 10:12.

O'Brien, S. J., and Johnson, W. E. 2005. Big cat genomics. Annual Review of Genomics and Human Genetics, 6: 407-429.

O'Brien, S. J., and Johnson, W. E. 2007. The evolution of cats. Scientific American. 297 (1): 68-75.

Odden, M.; Athreya, V.; Rattan, S.; and Linnell, J. D. 2014. Adaptable neighbours: movement patterns of GPS-collared leopards in human dominated landscapes in India. PLoS One, 9(11): e112044.

Seidensticker, J. 1976. On the ecological separation between tigers and leopards. Biotropica: 225-234.

da Silva, L. G. 2017. Ecology and Evolution of Melanism in Big Cats: Case Study with Black Leopards and Jaguars, in Big Cats. IntechOpen. https://www.intechopen.com/books/big-cats/ecology-and-evolution-of-melanism-in-big-cats-case-study-with-black-leopards-and-jaguars

Stein, A.B.; Athreya, V.; Gerngross, P.; Balme, G.; and others. 2016. Panthera pardus (errata version published in 2016). The IUCN Red List of Threatened Species 2016: e.T15954A102421779. https://www.iucnredlist.org/species/15954/102421779

Sunquist, M. and Sunquist, F. 2002. Wild Cats of the World. Chicago and London: University of Chicago Press. Retrieved from https://play.google.com/store/books/details?id=IF8nDwAAQBAJ

Turner, A., and Antón, M. 1997. The Big Cats and Their Fossil Relatives: An Illustrated Guide to Their Evolution and Natural History. New York: Columbia University Press.

Uphyrkina, O.; Johnson, W. E.; Quigley, H.; Miquelle, D.; and others. 2001. Phylogenetics, genome diversity and origin of modern leopard, Panthera pardus. Molecular Ecology, 10(11): 2617-2633.

Werdelin, L.; Yamaguchi, N.; Johnson, W. E.; and O'Brien, S. J. 2010. Phylogeny and evolution of cats (Felidae), in Biology and Conservation of Wild Felids, eds. Macdonald, D. W., and Loveridge, A. J., 59-82. Oxford: Oxford University Press.

Werdelin, L., and Dehghani, R. 2011. Carnivora, in Paleontology and Geology of Laetoli: Human Evolution in Context, Volume 2: Fossil Hominins and the Associated Fauna, Harrison, T., ed., 189-232. Springer, Dordrecht.

Wibisono, H. T.; Wahyudi, H. A.; Wilianto, E.; Pinondang, I. M. R.; and others. 2018. Identifying priority conservation landscapes and actions for the Critically Endangered Javan leopard in Indonesia: Conserving the last large carnivore in Java Island. PloS one, 13(6): e0198369.

Wikipedia. 2019. Leopard. https://en.wikipedia.org/wiki/Leopard Last accessed August 13, 2019.

Cat Specialist Group. 2019. Jaguar. http://www.catsg.org/index.php?id=95 Last accessed August 25, 2019.

Cavalcanti, S. C.; Marchini, S.; Zimmermann, A.; Gese, E. M.; and Macdonald, D. W. 2010. Jaguars, livestock, and people in Brazil: realities and perceptions behind the conflict, in Biology and Conservation of Wild Felids, eds. Macdonald, D. W., and Loveridge, A. J., 383-402. Oxford: Oxford University Press.

Culver, M.; Driscoll, C.; Eizirik, E.; and Spong, G. 2010. Genetic applications in wild felids, in Biology and Conservation of Wild Felids, ed. Macdonald, D. W., and Loveridge, A. J., 107-124. Oxford: Oxford University Press.

Eizirik, E.; Kim, J. H.; Menotti-Raymond, M.; Crawshaw Jr, P. G.; and others. 2001. Phylogeography, population history and conservation genetics of jaguars (Panthera onca, Mammalia, Felidae). Molecular Ecology, 10(1): 65-79.

Eizirik, E.; Yuhki, N.; Johnson, W. E.; Menotti-Raymond, M.; Hannah, S. S.; and O'Brien, S. J. 2003. Molecular genetics and evolution of melanism in the cat family. Current Biology. 13: 448-453.

Figueiró, H. V.; Li, G.; Trindade, F. J.; Assis, J.; and others. 2017. Genome-wide signatures of complex introgression and adaptive evolution in the big cats. Science Advances, 3(7): e1700299.

Ewer, R. F. 1973. The carnivores. The World Naturalist, ed. Carrington, R. London: Weidenfeld and Nicolson.

Figueiró, H. V.; Li, G.; Trindade, F. J.; Assis, J.; and others. 2017. Genome-wide signatures of complex introgression and adaptive evolution in the big cats. Science Advances, 3(7), e1700299.

Johnson, W. E.; Eizirik, E.; Pecon-Slattery, J.; Murphy, W. J.; and others. 2006. The Late Miocene radiation of modern Felidae: A genetic assessment. Science, 311:73-77.

Kitchener, A. C.; Van Valkenburgh, B.; and Yamaguchi, N. 2010. Felid form and function, in Biology and Conservation of Wild Felids, ed. Macdonald, D. W., and Loveridge, A. J., 83-106. Oxford: Oxford University Press.

Kitchener, A. C.; Breitenmoser-Würsten, C.; Eizirik, E.; Gentry, A.; and others. 2017. A revised taxonomy of the Felidae: The final report of the Cat Classification Task Force of the IUCN Cat Specialist Group. https://repository.si.edu/bitstream/handle/10088/32616/A_revised_Felidae_Taxonomy_CatNews.pdf

Li, G.; Figueiró, H. V.; Eizirik, E.; and Murphy, W. J. 2019. Recombination-aware phylogenomics reveals the structured genomic landscape of hybridizing cat species. Molecular Biology and Evolution. https://academic.oup.com/mbe/advance-article-pdf/doi/10.1093/molbev/msz139/28824386/msz139.pdf

Martin, L. D., and Neuner, A. M. 1978. The end of the Pleistocene in America. Transactions of the Nebraska Academy of Sciences and Affiliated Societies, 337. https://digitalcommons.unl.edu/cgi/viewcontent.cgi?article=1336&context=tnas Last accessed November 26, 2019.

Moreno, A. K. M., and Lima-Ribeiro, M. S. 2015. Ecological niche models, fossil record and the multi-temporal calibration for Panthera onca (Linnaeus, 1758)(Mammalia: Felidae). Brazilian Journal of Biological Sciences, 2(4): 309-319.

Macdonald, D. W.; Loveridge, A. J.; and Nowell, K. 2010. Dramatis personae: An introduction to the wild felids, in Biology and Conservation of Wild Felids, eds. Macdonald, D. W., and Loveridge, A. J., 3-58. Oxford: Oxford University Press.

Macdonald, D. W.; Loveridge, A. J.; and Rabinowitz, A. 2010a. Felid futures: crossing disciplines, borders, and generations, in Biology and Conservation of Wild Felids, eds. Macdonald, D. W., and Loveridge, A. J., 599-649. Oxford: Oxford University Press.

Nyakatura, K., and Bininda-Emonds, O. R. P. 2012. Updating the evolutionary history of Carnivora (Mammalia): a new species-level supertree complete with divergence time estimates. BMC Biology, 10:12.

O'Brien, S. J., and Johnson, W. E. 2005. Big cat genomics. Annual Review of Genomics and Human Genetics, 6: 407-429.

O'Brien, S. J., and Johnson, W. E. 2007. The evolution of cats. Scientific American, 297 (1): 68-75.

Quigley, H.; Foster, R.; Petracca, L.; Payan, E.; and others. 2017. Panthera onca (errata version published in 2018). The IUCN Red List of Threatened Species 2017: e.T15953A123791436.
https://www.iucnredlist.org/species/15953/123791436

San Diego Zoo. 2019. Jaguar: Panthera onca.
https://animals.sandiegozoo.org/animals/jaguar Last accessed November 25, 2019.

Schultz, C. B.; Martin, L. D.; and Schultz, M. R. 1984. A Pleistocene jaguar from North-Central Nebraska. Transactions of the Nebraska Academy of Sciences and Affiliated Societies, 228.
https://digitalcommons.unl.edu/cgi/viewcontent.cgi?article=1227&context=tnas Last accessed November 26, 2019.

Smith, F. A.; Tomé, C. P.; Elliott Smith, E. A.; Lyons, S. K.; and others. 2016. Unraveling the consequences of the terminal Pleistocene megafauna extinction on mammal community assembly. Ecography, 39(2): 223-239.

Sunquist, M. and Sunquist, F. 2002. Wild Cats of the World. Chicago and London: University of Chicago Press. Retrieved from
https://play.google.com/store/books/details?id=IF8nDwAAQBAJ

Thapa, K; Wikramanayake, E; Malla, S; Acharya, K. P.; and others. 2017
Tigers in the Terai: Strong evidence for meta-population dynamics
contributing to tiger recovery and conservation in the Terai Arc Landscape.
PLoS ONE 12(6): e0177548.

Turner, A., and Antón, M. 1997. The Big Cats and Their Fossil Relatives:
An Illustrated Guide to Their Evolution and Natural History. New York:
Columbia University Press.

Werdelin, L.; Yamaguchi, N.; Johnson, W. E.; and O'Brien, S. J. 2010.
Phylogeny and evolution of cats (Felidae), in Biology and Conservation of
Wild Felids, eds. Macdonald, D. W., and Loveridge, A. J., 59-82. Oxford:
Oxford University Press.

Werdelin, L., and Dehghani, R. 2011. Carnivora, in Paleontology and
Geology of Laetoli: Human Evolution in Context, Volume 2: Fossil Hominins
and the Associated Fauna, Harrison, T., ed., 189-232. Springer, Dordrecht.

Wikipedia. 2019. Jaguar. Last accessed November 26, 2019.

___. 2019. Jaguars in Mesoamerican culture.
https://en.wikipedia.org/wiki/Jaguars_in_Mesoamerican_cultures Last
accessed August 28, 2019.

___. 2019. Panthera gombaszoegensis.
https://en.wikipedia.org/wiki/Panthera_gombaszoegensis Last accessed
November 15, 2019.

Cat Specialist Group. 2019. Snow leopard.
http://www.catsg.org/index.php?id=100 Last accessed May 17, 2019.

Cho, Y. S.; Hu, L.; Hou, H.; Lee, H.; and others. 2013. The tiger genome and comparative analysis with lions and snow leopard genomes. Nature Communications, 4:24-33.

Christiansen, P. 2008. Phylogeny of the great cats (Felidae: Pantherinae), and the influence of fossil taxa and missing characters. Cladistics, 24(6): 977-992.

Ewer, R. F. 1973. The carnivores. The World Naturalist, ed. Carrington, R. London: Weidenfeld and Nicolson.

Gradstein, F. M.; Ogg, J. G.; and Hilgen, F. G. 2012. On the geologic time scale. Newsletters on Stratigraphy. 45(2): 171-188.

Heptner, V. G., and Sludskii, A. A. 1972. Mammals of the Soviet Union, volume II, part 2: Carnivora (hyaenas and cats). Moscow: Vysshaya Shkola Publishers. English translation by Rao, P.M., 1992. General editor: Kothekar, V. S. New Delhi: Amerind Publishing.
https://archive.org/details/mammalsofsov221992gept

Jackson, R. M.; Mishra, C.; McCarthy, T. M.; and Ale, S. B. 2010. Snow *leopards: conflict and conservation, in Biology and Conservation of Wild Felids, eds. Macdonald, D. W., and Loveridge, A. J., 417-430. Oxford: Oxford University Press.*

Johnson, W. E.; Eizirik, E.; Pecon-Slattery, J.; Murphy, W. J.; and others. 2006. The Late Miocene radiation of modern Felidae: A genetic assessment. Science, 311:73-77.

Kitchener, A. C.; Van Valkenburgh, B.; and Yamaguchi, N. 2010. Felid form and function, in Biology and Conservation of Wild Felids, ed. Macdonald, D. W., and Loveridge, A. J., 83-106. Oxford: Oxford University Press.

Kitchener, A. C.; Breitenmoser-Würsten, C.; Eizirik, E.; Gentry, A.; and others. 2017. A revised taxonomy of the Felidae: The final report of the Cat Classification Task Force of the IUCN Cat Specialist Group. https://repository.si.edu/bitstream/handle/10088/32616/A_revised_Felidae_Taxonomy_CatNews.pdf

Macdonald, D. W.; Loveridge, A. J.; and Nowell, K. 2010. Dramatis personae: An introduction to the wild felids, in Biology and Conservation of Wild Felids, eds. Macdonald, D. W., and Loveridge, A. J., 3-58. Oxford: Oxford University Press.

McCarthy, T.; Mallon, D.; Jackson, R.; Zahler, P.; and McCarthy, K. 2017. Panthera uncia. The IUCN Red List of Threatened Species 2017: e.T22732A50664030. https://www.iucnredlist.org/species/22732/50664030

Nyakatura, K., and Bininda-Emonds, O. R. P. 2012. *Updating the evolutionary history of Carnivora (Mammalia): a new species-level supertree complete with divergence time estimates. BMC Biology, 10:12.*

O'Brien, S. J., and Johnson, W. E. 2007. *The evolution of cats. Scientific American, 297 (1): 68-75.*

Sunquist, M. and Sunquist, F. 2002. *Wild Cats of the World. Chicago and London: University of Chicago Press. Retrieved from https://play.google.com/store/books/details?id=IF8nDwAAQBAJ*

Tseng, Z. J.; Wang, X.; Slater, G. J.; Takeuchi, G. T.; and others. 2014. *Himalayan fossils of the oldest known pantherine establish ancient origin of big cats. Proceedings of the Royal Society B: Biological Sciences, 281(1774): 20132686.*

Turner, A., and Antón, M. 1997. *The Big Cats and Their Fossil Relatives: An Illustrated Guide to Their Evolution and Natural History. New York: Columbia University Press.*

Wang, X.; Wang, Y.; Li, Q.; Tseng, J.; and others. 2015. *Cenozoic vertebrate evolution and paleoenvironment in Tibetan Plateau: Progress and prospects. Gondwana Research, 27: 1335-1354.*

Werdelin, L.; Yamaguchi, N.; Johnson, W. E.; and O'Brien, S. J. 2010.

Phylogeny and evolution of cats (Felidae), in Biology and Conservation of Wild Felids, eds. Macdonald, D. W., and Loveridge, A. J., 59-82. Oxford: Oxford University Press.

Wikipedia. 2019. Snow leopard.
https://en.wikipedia.org/wiki/Snow_leopard Last accessed May 17, 2019.

Clouded leopards:

Allen, M. L.; Wittmer, H. U.; Setiawan, E.; Jaffe, S.; and Marshall, A. J. 2016. Scent marking in Sunda clouded leopards (Neofelis diardi): novel observations close a key gap in understanding felid communication behaviours. Scientific Reports, 6: 35433.

Cat Specialist Group: Mainland and Sunda clouded leopards. http://www.catsg.org/index.php?id=116 and http://www.catsg.org/index.php?id=225. Last accessed September 17, 2017.

Christiansen, P. 2008. Evolutionary changes in craniomandibular shape in the great cats (Neofelis Griffith and Panthera Oken). Biological Journal of the Linnaean Society. 95:766-788.

___. 2008a. Phylogeny of the great cats (Felidae: Pantherinae), and the influence of fossil taxa and missing characters. Cladistics, 24(6): 977-992.

___. 2008b. Species distinction and evolutionary differences in the clouded leopard (Neofelis nebulosa) and Diard's clouded leopard (Neofelis diardi). Journal of Mammalogy, 89(6): 1435-1446.

Culver, M.; Driscoll, C.; Eizirik, E.; and Spong, G. 2010. Genetic applications in wild felids, in Biology and Conservation of Wild Felids, ed. D. W.

Macdonald and A. J. Loveridge, 107-123. Oxford: Oxford University Press, Oxford.

Ewer, R. F. 1973. The carnivores. The World Naturalist, ed. Carrington, R. London: Weidenfeld and Nicolson.

Grassman, L.; Lynam, A.; Mohamad, S.; Duckworth, J.W.; and others. 2016. Neofelis nebulosa. The IUCN Red List of Threatened Species 2016: e.T14519A97215090. https://www.iucnredlist.org/species/14519/97215090 Last accessed September 24, 2019.

Haidir, I. A.; Dinata, Y.; Linkie, M.; and Macdonald, D. W. 2013. Asiatic golden cat and Sunda clouded leopard occupancy in the Kerinci Seblat landscape, West-Central Sumatra. Cat News, 59: 7-10.

Hearn, A.; Ross, J.; Brodie, J.; Cheyne, S.; and others. 2015. Neofelis diardi (errata version published in 2016). The IUCN Red List of Threatened Species 2015: e.T136603A97212874 https://www.iucnredlist.org/species/136603/97212874

Heptner, V. G., and Sludskii, A. A. 1972. Mammals of the Soviet Union, volume II, part 2: Carnivora (hyaenas and cats). Moscow: Vysshaya Shkola Publishers. English translation by Rao, P.M., 1992. General editor: Kothekar, V. S. New Delhi: Amerind Publishing. https://archive.org/details/mammalsofsov221992gept

Johnson, W. E.; Eizirik, E.; Pecon-Slattery, J.; Murphy, W. J.; and others. 2006. The Late Miocene Radiation of Modern Felidae: A Genetic Assessment. Science, 311:73-77.

Kitchener, A. C.; Van Valkenburgh, B.; and Yamaguchi, N. 2010. Felid form and function, in Biology and Conservation of Wild Felids, ed. Macdonald, D. W., and Loveridge, A. J., 83-106. Oxford: Oxford University Press.

Kitchener, A. C.; Breitenmoser-Würsten, C.; Eizirik, E.; Gentry, A.; and others. 2017. A revised taxonomy of the Felidae: The final report of the Cat Classification Task Force of the IUCN Cat Specialist Group. https://repository.si.edu/bitstream/handle/10088/32616/A_revised_Felida e_Taxonomy_CatNews.pdf

Lee, S. 2017. Move to protect the Sunda clouded leopard. The Star. http://www.thestar.com.my/news/nation/2017/06/12/move-to-protect-the -sunda-clouded-leopard/#iQuVGjP6h94qzKT2.01 Last accessed September 17, 2017.

Macdonald, D. W.; Loveridge, A. J.; and Nowell, K. 2010. Dramatis personae: an introduction to the wild felids, in Biology and Conservation of Wild Felids, ed. D. W. Macdonald and A. J. Loveridge, 3-58. Oxford: Oxford University Press, Oxford.

Nyakatura, K., and Bininda-Emonds, O. R. P. 2012. Updating the evolutionary history of Carnivora (Mammalia): a new species-level supertree complete with divergence time estimates. BMC Biology. 10:12.

O'Brien, S. J., and Johnson, W. E. 2007. The evolution of cats. Scientific American. 297 (1):68-75.

de Queiroz, K. 2007. Species concepts and species delimitation. Systematic Biology, 56(6): 879-886.

Ridout, M. S., and Linkie, M. 2009. Estimating overlap of daily activity patterns from camera trap data. Journal of Agricultural, Biological, and Environmental Statistics, 14(3): 322-337.

Sunquist, M. and Sunquist, F. 2002. Wild Cats of the World. Chicago and London: University of Chicago Press. Retrieved from https://play.google.com/store/books/details?id=IF8nDwAAQBAJ

Tan, C. K. W.; Rocha, D. G.; Clements, G. R.; Brenes-Mora, E.; and others. 2017. Habitat use and predicted range for the mainland clouded leopard Neofelis nebulosa in Peninsular Malaysia. Biological Conservation, 206: 65-74.

Werdelin, L., and Olsson, L. 1997. How the leopard got its spots: a phylogenetic view off the evolution of felid coat patterns. Biological Journal of the Linnaen Society. 62:383-400.

Werdelin, L.; Yamaguchi, N.; Johnson, W. E.; and O'Brien, S. J.. 2010. Phylogeny and evolution of cats (Felidae), in Biology and Conservation of

Wild Felids, eds. Macdonald, D. W., and Loveridge, A. J., 59-82. Oxford: Oxford University Press.

Wikipedia. 2019. Mainland and Sunda clouded leopards. https://en.wikipedia.org/wiki/Clouded_leopard and https://en.wikipedia.org/wiki/Sunda_clouded_leopard Last accessed September 24, 2019.

Wilting, A.; Christiansen, P.; Kitchener, A. C.; Kemp, Y. J. M.; and others. 2011. Geographical variation in and evolutionary history of the Sunda clouded leopard (Neofelis diardi) (Mammalia: Carnivora: Felidae) with the description of a new subspecies from Borneo. Molecular Phylogenetics and Evolution, 58: 317-328.

www.ingramcontent.com/pod-product-compliance
Lightning Source LLC
Chambersburg PA
CBHW031108250726
48655CB00004B/1634